To Chuck Vetter:
If at first you don't retire —
try, try again.

Joseph Schwartz

DON'T EVER RETIRE
BUT
DO IT EARLY
AND
OFTEN

DON'T EVER RETIRE
BUT
DO IT EARLY
AND
OFTEN

by
JOSEPH SCHWARTZ

FARNSWORTH PUBLISHING CO., INC.
Rockville Centre, New York 11570

© 1979, Joseph Schwartz.
All rights reserved.
First printing, July 1979.
Published by Farnsworth Publishing Co., Inc.
Rockville Centre, New York 11570.
Library of Congress Catalog Card No. 79-53374.
ISBN 0-87863-196-8.
Manufactured in the United States of America.
No part of this book may be reproduced
without the written permission of the publisher.

THIS BOOK IS DEDICATED TO
my wife, Agnes, naturally.

Table of Contents

PAGE

FOREWORD by Howard Jarvis   1

PROLOGUE   5

CHAPTER
    I.   FIRST, I AM GOING TO TELL YOU   9
         what I am going to tell you

    II. LIFE EXPECTANCY   19
         just keep breathing as long as you live

    III. YOUR JOB   25
         is this really what you want to do forever?

    IV. PRE-RETIREMENT FEARS   33
         why worry—you might not get there

    V. FINANCIAL PLANNING   39
         best to live to spend

    VI. NO ONE NEED FEAR BOREDOM   55
         when someone needs someone

    VII. COLLECT SOCIAL SECURITY   63
         no need to wait for your brother

    VIII LOOK FORWARD TO RETIREMENT OR
         DREAD IT   71
         but find out why

    IX. EXECUTIVES RETIRE, TOO   79
         sooner or later

X. AFTER RETIREMENT   87
    go to work so you can retire again

XI. STAY ON DAYLIGHT SAVING TIME   95
     and loosen your shoelaces

XII. A COUPLE WILL BE A SINGLE SOMEDAY   101
      because it's only temporary, never permanent

XIII. A WIDOWER HAS A CHOICE   107
       for he can be a couple any day

XIV. A WOMAN HAS A CHOICE   113
      unless she prefers not to

XV. AGE DISCRIMINATION   121
     or living in an age of stupidity

XVI. MANDATORY RETIREMENT AT AGE 65
      OR 70   129
      much ado about nothing

XVII. THE SINGLE HOME AND THE SENIOR   137
       can you afford to live in your own home?

XVIII. RETIREMENT COMMUNITIES   147
        disneyland for seniors

XIX. MOBILE HOMES   155
      retirement community parking lots

XX. I N F L A T I O N   161
     as long as you like it

XXI. SENIOR CITIZENS FLEX THEIR MUSCLES 171
      move over—we want it all, too

XXII. FEAR OF PHYSICAL DISABILITY   181
       best be rich or be poor

XXIII INSTANT CREDIT CARD   187
       a tax-sheltered health care plan for life

XXIV   NOW I AM GOING TO TELL YOU   207
       what I told you

       EPILOGUE   215

       INDEX   217

FOREWORD
by
Howard Jarvis

A few years ago, I had the privilege of writing the Foreword for a new book. I had known the author, Joseph Schwartz, only a short time, but I was impressed with his sincerity of expression. And I recall predicting that "if this man can write like he talks—authoritative, yet humble; complicated, yet simplistic; serious, yet humorous; consoling, yet provocative—he is destined to be recognized as an author of note."

That book was not meant for the general public, as it dealt with the cold facts and figures of the economics of owning and operating apartment buildings. But it read like a fictional love story; the love and care for a building as though it were a piece of art; and the humanistic treatment of its residents, as though tenants were members of his family. The book was accepted by thousands, who found that it added a new dimension of social significance to the heretofore impersonal investment field.

Since then I have gotten to know Joe well, and I learned that he has a mission in life. He is an angry man. Or to state it more accurately, he is angry AT MAN, because we are not utilizing our greatest national resource—the mature segment of our nation. Schwartz claims, that MAN, at the peak of his ability, mentality and expertise is allowed, expected, encouraged and forced to discontinue his productive efforts; and he says that the greater shame belongs to MAN, who has accepted the doctrine that when he reaches society's retirement age; he retires into oblivion.

I believe that Schwartz's mission accomplished book— DON'T EVER RETIRE *BUT* DO IT EARLY AND OFTEN, will be hailed as one of the most important books of our time.

Months before publication date I was so impressed with his solution to one of our major national problems, that I wrote him as follows:

"I urge you to release Chapter XXIII of your book NOW before publication, as I consider your charge card plan for funding Health Care most vital to our economy.
The use of Tax Shelters as a benefit for all citizenry is ingenious.
I am pleased to endorse the Federal Medical Charge Card Plan, as it is a tremendous step forward in political responsibility."

In my opinion, this book will have a most beneficial effect on our men and women, of all ages, and it can be of lasting benefit to the stability of our country. We cannot afford to continue to waste the productive capabilities of those among us who have been God-blessed with more years lived than most—and with many more useful years to live.

Howard Jarvis

Howard Jarvis, of Proposition 13 fame, is probably the most famous senior citizen in the nation. Even his most outspoken critics will acknowledge the tremendous impact this dynamic septuagenarian has had and continues to have on the economy of the United States.

PROLOGUE

In 1956, my wife and I joined with nine other middle-aged couples to form a stock investment club to pool our funds and invest collectively—for 20 heads are better than one. Tennet Associates was our name, and making money in the stock market was our game.

We began with monthly meetings at members' homes, each couple contributing $25 to the investment fund. Everyone had a say in what stocks we purchased. We bought on tips from Uncle Louie, overhearances at beauty parlors, and sometimes after reading a financial report. Since our stock portfolio began to show ever increasing profits, we increased our monthly contribution to $50—and once in a while, assessed members an additional $100 to finance a "hot tip" that just couldn't miss. We also went through four different stock broker advisors (went through means we took their advice before giving up on them), but none of them knew what they were doing. (I take that back—they did know what they were doing—they sold the stuff to us.)

Our original group of 10 middle-aged couples has now dwindled to eight older aged couples, but we are still going strong—socially, that is—not financially. For to tell the truth, we were never an outstanding example as an investment group, and our stocks today are only worth about 35% of our original investment. Of course there were moments when we were ahead of Wall Street. But who can get 20 people to agree to sell when you are making money? And when you're losing—it's stupid to sell, isn't it?

And not one of us has really made a profit overall on our *personal* stock portfolio over the same 23 year period. But every member had purchased a home, or an apartment building, or a commercial building, or acreage—and in every case, the property or land has appreciated substantially over the same 23 year period. So I must conclude that the stock market is not as sure a route to financial security as housing and land.

Time has taken its toll of our Tennet Associates. Two of our male members and one woman member have died. And those of us who have survived have all reached, or are about to reach, or have passed the prescribed age of retirement. And as we grew older, I noticed that everyone viewed retirement differently—some were worrying about it and some said they were looking forward to retirement.

We began to discuss retirement and we read everything we could find on the subject. We discovered many new books on "aging gracefully" and "life in the good *older* days." Most of the writings tried to convince us that we were not senile and useless—but we knew that already. Then there are the best sellers that try to boost our spirits by telling us that sexual activity at age 70 is better than at age 40. Of course it is! When a 70 year old man has sexual intercourse, he puts more zest into it because he is always aware it might be his last time. And what about "the amazing earth shaking secret revealed for the first time in the book that tells it all?" All you really learn there is that a man over 70, or even over 80, would if he could and usually can, and that a woman of that age could and usually would. Big deal!

Can you imagine how many copies would be sold if a doctor wrote a book recommending that men over age 60 should be sex surrogates for *young women.* Come to think of it—makes sense at that. It would not only relieve the problem of boredom for older men but also enhance the status of the aged. My guess is that a book fostering this premise would probably outsell ROOTS.

But getting down to serious business, we are tired of being told that men and women in their 70's, 80's, and even 90's are productive, successful, exemplary, and happy. We're fed up with being compared to Bob Hope, Mae West, George Burns, Lawrence Welk, Artur Rubinstein, Marlene Dietrich, and an assortment of 86 year old marathon runners, supreme court judges, mountain climbers and belly dancers. What about some of the non-celebrities for a change? Hell, there are more of us than there are of them. What about a book that treats older folks as normal average people with the same needs and problems older folks have experienced for generations on end, and some good ideas for solving some of these problems?

We are not freaks; we are not to be pitied; we are not outcasts; we are not a burden to society. Without us there would be no society.

We are the strongest, the best, the fittest, the cream of our nation—for we are the survivors of the youth of our generation.

We eat, we sleep, we work, we dream, we love, we lust, we laugh—we are men and women possessing the wisdom and experience of survival—JUST LIKE YOU WILL BE, IF YOU SURVIVE THE YOUTH OF YOUR DAY—and that is how we want to be treated.

CHAPTER I

FIRST, I AM GOING TO TELL YOU

what I am going to tell you

This is not a technical retirement text with comprehensive statistics, actuarial tables, or magic get rich formulae. I will be short on figures, but long on people. Figures will change in years to come, but people won't. This is a people book on how to view retirement; how to plan your retirement; and what to do when you retire and—that's right—how to retire more often more enjoyably!

* * * * * * * * * * * * * *

I am not going to tell you how to get rich quick and retire.

I am going to tell you why retiring quick will enrich you.

* * * * * * * * * * * * *

I am not going to tell you how to retire on welfare.

I am going to tell you why to retire *for* your own welfare.

* * * * * * * * * * * * *

I am not going to tell you that retirement is the golden years ; serene years ; restful years ; leisure years ; or the best years of your life.

I am going to tell you how to prevent retirement from being the lousiest years of your life.

* * * * * * * * * * * *

I am not going to tell you that retirement at 65 means you have only a few more years to live.

I am going to tell you that retirement can be 30% or more of your entire life span.

* * * * * * * * * * * * *

I am not going to tell you about retirement as an end.

I am going to tell you about retirement as a beginning.

* * * * * * * * * * * * *

I will emphasize again and again that retirement should not mean inactivity. It should, instead, be a change from what you are working at, to what you would most enjoy doing. For money or for fun—or best yet—for money and fun.

This book is directed mainly to the executive and middle-income class. The wealthy don't need nor want my advice, for they have always been retired. And the poor might resent it, for I have no magic formula to improve their financial situation. But the middle-income class is a large and largely ignored segment of our population, and I mainly address my writing to them because they are the ones I think I can help.

One cannot discuss retirement without dealing with pensions. We must realize that we are living in a crazy giveaway era and in a society that right or wrong, is making unbridled demands for ever-increasing pensions, which can bankrupt the country and destroy what is left of our now half-enslaved free enterprise system. We must recognize the danger, and acknowledge that no society can exist when its nonproductive population outnumbers its producers, and that day is almost here.

But I am also a realist. So there is no cause for our generation to worry or fear. *The young may have been born too late,* but *we* still have time to get a free ride on the bandwagon. So don't be thick skulled or heroic. Get on now and get a longer ride, while early retirement is still allowed.

* * * * * * * * * * * * * *

I wish there were another word for *retirement* than retirement. For although this book is about retirement, it is not about the kind of retirement that is defined in the dictionary.

All researchers and writers on this subject have hopes of inventing a new term that would be more applicable, but no one has yet been able to come up with an acceptable substitute. So although I dislike the words *retire* and *retirement* and disagree with their definitions, I must use those terms throughout this book, otherwise my writing would be ambiguous.

    Look up "retire" in your dictionary. The definition is
        "to withdraw from business" or
        "to withdraw from public life" or
        "to withdraw from danger" or
        "no longer qualified for active service."

    It all adds up to OUT OF ACTION—to become INACTIVE.

    And the definition for "retirement" naturally follows as the "state of being retired."

    These definitions are completely false and have no application to PEOPLE as they are dealt with in this book. Inactive retirement of people is neither a normal nor healthy state of existence.

    Retirement (withdrawal from productive life) of people is a phenomenon of our urbanized industrial system. It is an absurd 20th century custom whose only outcome could be to bankrupt the economy of the future generations of the society that created it. (Nor is this statement affected by changing the mandatory retirement from age 65 to age 70.) Inactivity or non-production cannot be economically justified since, economically, no society can afford it.

    The normal, natural, economic rule of human life is that people should be productive all their *productive* life. Doesn't the claimed fact that farmers outlive all other occupational groups tend to confirm this contention? And please don't jump to conclusions. I would be the last one to say that a person should perform manual labor until the end of his life.

I once attended a seminar on Gerontology (the study of aging) where a Chinese lady was asked, "What is the word for 'retirement' in the Chinese language?"

She answered, "There is no word for retirement. Chinese people believe one should work as long as one is able. Retirement is the same as 'death' in the Chinese language."

This is what I hope to convey. The dictionary definition of retirement might as well be "death." The correct definition should be

"a time when one leaves his work or gives up his position to do whatever he wishes, whenever he wishes."

It might be work and play, or play at work. And it can be a long time, for 30% of your lifetime or longer.

I am surprised that no dictionary, to my knowledge, has ever defined *retire* as "to change a tire." I could accept such a definition, for that would be in keeping with my philosophy—to change from the old to the new.

And since I am dealing with definitions, and since I am conscious and respectful of women's rights, I promise to use the term "person" whenever possible, and my use of "he" or "his" is meant to be "he/she" and "his/hers" whenever applicable. But I also promise that when I say "she" or "hers," I do not mean "he" or "his."

* * * * * * * * * * * * *

Consider this simple axiom. A SELF-EMPLOYED PERSON (with no employees) is a RETIRED PERSON. A person who has been self-employed all his productive life HAS BEEN RETIRED ALL HIS LIFE! It is something to ponder.

Any person who can, without need of prior notice or

permission, change his hours of work by his own decision is self-employed. And any such self-employed person is retired, for he can work when he wants to, as hard as he wants to, and loaf when he wants to.

It is time to formally change the established dictionary definition of "retirement" by confining this definition to *things or objects*. When a machine tool becomes obsolete, or an article of clothing becomes threadbare, it goes to the scrap heap, is put out of action, and is retired. But not people.

The surge of interest in, and study of the problems of, aging by the Geronotologists, the AARP, the Gray Panthers, and many enlightened persons of all ages, are to be credited with our refusal to accept the "scrap heap" definition.

So whenever I speak of retirement I am not referring to the "rocking chair age" definition but to a "work menopause."

J.H. is an outstanding example of the way I interpret retirement.

NOTE: Initials used in Profiles are fictitious in order to protect the innocent—especially the author.

PROFILE OF J.H.

Retired at age 31, financially secure; retired again in 1942, not quite as well-off; again in 1945, better-off; and again in 1964 at age 60, with financial resources spelling independence for life.

The above covered a myriad of occupations from newspaper publishing to manufacturing; from no employees to 13,000 employees; from zero resources to financial security.

From age 60 to 70, J.H. devoted full time, without pay, exhorting anyone and everyone to enlist in a fight against City Hall! Now everyone knows that you can't beat City Hall—everyone but J.H. So he was the pesky old fuss-budget who showed up at the city, county, and state legislative meetings to voice his protest. The TV cameras covered his appearances for he was always good for a Will Rogers type of quote, although often requiring censorship.

In 1974, at age 70, he retired one more time to a full-time salaried position as executive director of an old run-down, financially tottering trade association. Since the salary wasn't too secure (in fact, it wasn't available for a year or two) it was agreed that J.H. could also maintain his no-pay amateur lobbyist functions.

Interesting—a 70 year old going down hill association and a 70 year old retiree joining forces. Result: in 5 years, the association is now the largest in its trade, and the retiree has not only licked City Hall but has become the symbol for national and international anti-bureacracy movements. (I dare say no more, or you might guess his identity.)

RATING BY J.S.: This man does not live in the past. He lives in the present and affects the future. He has been advised repeatedly to slow down, and he answers, "If you can get the clock to slow down, I'll slow down. Since time goes on and on, so must MAN. When my time ends, I'll slow down. Until then, run with me, or else get out of my way."

* * * * * * * * * * * * * * *

The cry for equality is loudest when tied to age and retirement. Who dares speak against housing, medical care, food stamps, bingo games and shuffle boards for the old folks? But don't depend on the equality advocates for your pre-retirement planning. Your retirement hopes and needs to achieve those hopes are uniquely yours—and yours alone. This is planning for the time when you can do your own thing —not the thing others want or expect you to do. What you want is not so much equality as the right to be yourself!

If it is true that all men are created equal, THAT IS
THE ONLY TIME THEY ARE EQUAL, the day they are
born. One moment after the first breath, the new human is
different—not equal. You cannot legislate equality, for no
person really wants to be equal. We all want to be better
than equal. To be equal means to be average, and who wants
to be average?

We used to accept the fact that every individual was
unique. Now it seems that our groupee-infested society
boisterously demands that our government should reshape
all individuals into unisex robots. Share and share alike.
An equal portion for all. Take away from those who have
and give to those who have not. No matter that those who
have, have earned what they have, and those who have not,
were unproductive!

I will share a secret with my readers. Mindless equality
is a political vote-getting fraud, unnatural, impractical, impossible. For if you divided all goods, food, and property
equally amongst all the people—within one hour (after the
shock had subsided) the state of equality would have been
shattered and we would once again have the beginning of
the making of the classic three degrees of affluence: the
rich, the middle-income class, and the poor. You cannot
legislate equality, so don't expect it at retirement.

* * * * * * * * * * * * * *

In the past, retirement never was the monumental problem it is becoming today. People got older and died without
the fuss we now make over the basic laws of nature. Grandma
never worried about rest homes, for she was resting in her
oldest daughter's home (which probably was Grandpa's while
he was alive).

But all that is passe and our family unit is out-dated.
It has been eliminated as old fashioned, unnecessary, im-

practical, and virtually immoral. In its place, we have created public schools as nannies for our young; churches as pacifiers for our parents; television as sweeteners for our culture; and government as The Almighty Saviour, responsible for our problems.

These man-made non-filial systems have taken over the responsibility of love and protection of the family unit, so that the individual no longer has the obligation to take care of his own.

I would not be surprised to hear of legislation proposed to make all parents wards of the State. Preposterous? Some may think so at first blush, but the reality is that thousands upon thousands are already wards of the State—and millions more are part-ward and part-free. Nor is this confined to parents and elderly, but applies also to singles and young.

In our society the family unit has been largely replaced by the unit of one: YOU and YOU alone! I can't change it. I guess too many people like it that way.

The fact is that no one but you can prepare for the time in your life when you can practice self-survival with impunity, and when you can be truly as free as man can ever hope to be—and that time is retirement. For not until you retire from that which you *must* do, to that which you *want* to do, will you have the freedom we all yearn for.

As soon as you were born, you immediately began your life sentence of servitude. Your parents controlled what you could do and what you could not do. Then to school, and your teachers told you what to do. Then to work, and your employer told you. When you became free of your parents by getting married, your spouse took over and told you what to do.

But one day you will reach the magic age when you

are *expected* to retire from your job, and for the first time in your life you will be free because no one can tell you what to do. Even your wife will ease up because she will feel sorry for you. She knows that she will outlive you by eight years, so you can have it all your way from now on.

What a glorious time for those of you who still have one of your natural instincts left—the instinct of wanting to be free. No school teachers to regiment you; no minister, priest, rabbi, or guru to pester you; only the man-made Saviour called Government to restrain you and take from you some of your treasured possessions.

The reason so many of us are afraid of retirement is because we fear the unknown. We have all grown so accustomed to being directed all of our lives that we dread being free to make our own decisions. We are a horde of lost souls. We want to be told what to do. All right, so I'll TELL YOU: Make plans to retire earlier and live longer and happier. Don't wait until THEY tell you you're through. Choose the time for yourself and tell THEM you quit!

CHAPTER II

LIFE EXPECTANCY

just keep breathing as long as you live

There are mountains of books, booklets and articles that tell you "How To Grow Old," and in my opinion they are quite unnecessary, for it appears that the American public has already learned how. We are told that in the U.S. today one out of every ten is over 65 (over 22 million) and that by 2030 it will be one out of every six.

But the lesson seems to have been learned by women much better than by men. Fifty years ago there were almost an even ratio of men and women over age 65—100 men to 100 women. (Seems unbelievable, doesn't it? It is—don't believe it. I don't.) Today (again we are told) it is 69 men to 100 women over age 65, and by the year 2000, the Census Bureau Population Division projects a ratio of 65 men to 100 women.

However, I have a theory I defy anyone to disprove. And please remember, you never read or heard of this astounding theory before.

My theory is that the government conclusions that there is a tremendous increase in the over age 65 segment *as compared to 50 years ago* ARE ERRONEOUS. For prior to Social Security and Medicare, please NAME ONE ADVANTAGE IN REACHING AGE 65. I'll wait while you think . . . . Time's up. You could not think of one. Right? Our people always tended to fake their ages downward because of jobs, insurance, vanity, etc., but when Social Security, Medicare, and more generous public employee and industry pension plans came into being, our population suddenly became older as they lined to register their true ages.

I'm not the only one who thinks our government guesstimates are off base. Even our government official total population figure is in doubt. And its birth and death rates are questionable.

For example: The Environmental Fund (a private organization which was founded to study the problems of world population growth), released figures which were not in agreement with the U.S. figures.

The Fund claimed that the U.S. population was 6.5 million higher than the official government estimate.

It also claimed the death rate and the birth rate were lower than reported by the government.

* * * * * * * * * * * * * * *

Although I do not believe the *over age 65 comparative*

statistics of years ago, the trend towards an increasingly older population is indisputable. And women will outnumber men, for women have a longer life expectancy, according to the actuarial tables. (I wonder, did it start with Eve? Did Eve outlive Adam?) I am certain that scientists are studying the reasons for the "weaker sex" outliving the "stronger sex."

Medical advances have resulted in a reduction of infant mortality, and an extension of life so that older people have a longer retirement span. In 1900, the U.S. average life expectancy from birth was only 51 years for a girl baby, and 48 years for a boy baby.

More recent figures (1973 Expectation of Life At Birth) were 75 years for females and 67 for males; 1975 figures rose to 77 years for females and 69 years for males. (These figures are the averages for whites. Non-whites have had lower expectancies, however they have achieved even more dramatic increases of double their 1900 figures.)

But this does not mean that a woman (with a 77 year expectancy) who retires at age 65 will have only 12 years remaining. Nor that a man (with a 69 year expectancy) who retires at 65, will have only four more years to go. For the longer one lives, the more his or her life expectancy keeps increasing.

A woman who reaches age 65 has a life expectancy of 18 or more years—to age 83—because she has survived to age 65.

A man who reaches age 65 has a life expectancy of 14 more years—to age 79—because he has survived to age 65.

Too many people still believe that "three score and ten" is all one should expect, and that anyone living beyond age 70 is living on borrowed time. However, the life expectancy table on the following page shows that at age 70, both sexes can plan on cashing their Social Security checks through their 80th birthday—and then some.

1975 LIFE SPAN—as released by U.S. Department HEW

AT AGE	FEMALE Life Expectancy to AGE	MALE AGE
Birth	77	69
20	79	71
30	79	72
40	79	73
45	80	74
50	80	74
55	81	75
60	82	77
65	83	79
70	84	81
75	86	84
80	89	87
85	92	90

(adjusted for fractions of years to nearest year)

* * * * * * * * * * * * * *

I will now let you in on what this fuss is all about. Retirement can be a long living time, and you 65 year old boys (and girls) who make it to 79 (and 83), will find that you still have more time to serve. Because we must have many 90's to give us an average of 79 or 83.

So look at retirement NOT as a short period to endure, close to death—BUT a long period to live, a long way from death.

REMEMBER, YOUR RETIREMENT LIFE CAN EASILY BE 30% OR MORE OF YOUR ENTIRE LIFETIME.

The odds are in a retiree's favor. Your retirement life span can easily be a longer period than your youth. So don't fear retirement. Look forward to living it fully. For this could be the largest and most important part of your lifetime.

You must therefore agree that this book's theme, that you should retire earlier, is meaningful. For if you retire at age 60 or 62, you are sure to have more retirement years than if you waited until 65 or 70. If we assume that retirement can be a most satisfying phase of one's life—if not *the* most satisfying phase—you should plan to have more of it.

CHAPTER III

YOUR JOB

is this really what you want to do forever?

Many people perform the duties of their job with as much feeling as robots, and if they were polled as to whether or not they enjoyed their work, you would be surprised at the percentage who are indifferent, since they never thought of their job in that light. To most workers, a job is a paycheck, and that is all they expect from a job.

The worker who is ambitious for promotion is the worker most apt to be a job-hater. He feels that his talents are being wasted in his current duties and responsibilities. Surprisingly he is not usually dissatisfied with his income. His motivation is not to get more money but rather to move up to a higher job, which incidentally will provide more money, which is what makes it a "promotion." As he succeeds in moving up the ladder to supervision and then to management, he becomes more frustrated than ever, for middle-management personnel are the unhappiest of all working people.

Once in middle-management he will tell you that the blue collar workers are not interested in being more productive, a statement he knows to be true because he used to be one himself. And he will be the first to admit (off the record) that executives are inefficient and "gold-brickers." And if he suceeds in attaining executive rank, he is apt to do his own share of gold-bricking. But he will no longer be a job-hater. Instead he will probably become a mandatory retirement hater as he gets closer to age 65.

Through our progression from the simplicity, hardships, and fight for survival by living off the land, to the complexities of living off the production of others, we have come a long way, but not necessarily to a good end. The trend is that too many of us are opting to work in the service area (such as doctors, lawyers, public employees) and too few in the productive fields (such as farmers, carpenters, factory workers)—and an ever-increasing number in the do nothing area (such as welfare recipients and too many *actually retired* folks).

An example of Webster's definition of retirement is "the *rest* of the life" of W.F.

PROFILE OF W.F.

Retired at 55 forever.

This man did his pre-retirement planning carefully, thoroughly, and dishonestly. He studied the vertebral column, for he was preparing to fake a backache—not for just a day or two, but forever after.

He really got the idea when he was solicited for mortgage (life) insurance by the lending bank's insurance man. His house mortgage payments were $275 per month. The insurance salesman emphasized that the bank wanted him to buy mortage insurance so that if he were disabled or died, the amount of the mortgage would be paid-for by the insurance company—and they would not have to be the bad guys and foreclose. And W.F. already knew that his company pension plan provided for immediate pension payments in event of total disability. And he also knew that a backache was hard to disprove for he heard of a guy who had faked it for years.

W.F. did not buy any additional disability or life policies, for he was no dummy—insurance companies have noses and they can smell. He only bought the mortgage policy which he could prove that he did not seek—the bank aggressively solicited him. And after waiting a respectable time (2 years) he decided to test his plan.

W.F. was more than smart; as a chiseler he was brilliant. He reported to his company that he was unable to come to work due to an excruciating backache. He hinted that he thought he got hurt on the job, but he wasn't sure. Of course, there were X-rays, tests, doctors, etc., but W.F. was groaning and moaning for he was in awful pain as anyone could hear.

The company was anxious to settle with a nice loyal employee who wasn't claiming Workmen's Compensation, nor did he once mention that he was hiring an attorney to sue the company. Result—early disability retirement of $575 a month for life (unless he decides to recover).

And the mortgage insurance company investigated, examined, X-rayed—but the pain persisted. Result—W.F. no longer pays $275 monthly mortgage payments. So W.F. has been retired and faking for over five years, and getting away with it.

RATING BY J.S.: W.F. may think he is getting the best

of the deal, but in effect he is not, because he cannot do
many things he once enjoyed doing. He can't bowl or play
golf, and many of his former friends suspect he is a fraud.
His existence is furtive and nervous because he worries that
the insurance sleuths will get wise to him. He spends his
time doing nothing and, in my opinion, that's what he
amounts to—nothing.

* * * * * * * * * * * * * *

Every person is forced at an early age to make a decision
as to what work he is going to perform for his livelihood. At
the time he must make his choice, he is not capable of knowing what he is best suited for, nor what he would most enjoy.
And even if he does know, he often is unable to pursue the
occupation he most desires. Many who might enjoy painting,
music, writing, plumbing, carpentering, or doctoring, soon
discover that the price one must pay to achieve financial
rewards in those fields is too high or unattainable.

Many choose the occupation of their fathers who,
more likely than not, were never happy over their choice.

Many people are limited to the employment opportunities of their immediate surroundings, whether it be coal
mining, shoe manufacturing, or auto assembling. The world
is not every man's oyster. In many cases, boy meets girl—
boy wants to marry girl—boy needs money—boy gets a job,
any job that pays money—boy stays on job because he needs
the pay check.

I was a musician. I enjoyed my work but it was not a
steady every day occupation. I met a girl and wanted to get
married. So I took a job (the only job I could find in the depression of '32) selling life insurance. We had a son—I
couldn't give up my job, so I stayed in the life insurance business for 40 years until I retired early at age 62. Although I
did not dislike my work, I do know that it kept me from
doing that which I would have most enjoyed. And as proof,

I submit that I do not miss my insurance activities as I am so busy that I don't know how I ever had the time to go to work.

My son was sure he knew what he wanted to do for his life's work. He was going to be an actor, writer, and director. From age eight he studied and worked at acting. At age 13 he became associated with the Circle Theatre, a theatre in the round. A group of aspiring thespians transformed a run-down dilapidated store into a hand-me-down dilapidated theatre seating about 85. Alumni from this humble theater include such successful actors as Martin Strothers, Kathleen Freeman, Paul Sands, and a number of writers and directors—but my son was not one of those who chose to pay the price for success in this precarious field.

For my son Dan met *the* girl—wanted to get married—needed a regular income—so he took a job selling insurance. They had a daughter, and then another daughter, and he remained in the insurance industry for the past 25 years, progressing through the ranks to a top executive position. He is happy and he is successful. Perhaps he is happy because he is successful. But this book is written for him too. Hopefully he will one day retire earlier because of this book, and he too will from then on work at whatever he most enjoys doing. It might be the theatre but it might be insurance—that's up to him.

But don't forget that I listed a number of successful alumni. They attained financial security in the work they thought they most enjoyed. Even to them I suggest they plan to retire early—if there is some other work they ever thought they might like to do—try it. Selling insurance or real estate might be more fun at their later stage in life, and if not, and if acting is really their bag, they should continue ad infinitum.

For after-retirement is the time to work at whatever

one most enjoys—otherwise, WHEN?

* * * * * * * * * * * * * *

Some people don't realize that they are expected to retire—and that they did—but they didn't. And one who didn't was A.H.

PROFILE OF A.H.

Retired since 1932, or 1946, or 1965?

A.H. knew what he wanted to do since childhood. He wanted to blow a horn, make noise called music. And he succeeded, since he became a proficient musician earning the No. 1 spot in the brass section. Many of us have heard him play as a member of orchestras such as Hal Kemp, Ozzie Nelson, Fred Waring and on many radio and television musical hours.

A.H. had an ideal life, enjoying his work, happily married to his childhood sweetheart, and living in a cottage with a white picket fence. But music has its shortcomings—he told me, "I had so much leisure time, and I got so damn tired of cutting geraniums."

But that really wasn't his hangup. A.H. had two fears—his teeth and his hair. If he lost his teeth, he would not be able to make sweet sounds, and if he lost his hair, he would no longer be seated in the front row of the brass section. So he became a real estate salesman in 1946 as a sideline to his music and relaxed, since he knew it could one day become his main line. He prospered in both lines and became known as the musicians' realtor. This naturally lead to his owning and operating apartment buildings—and selling and managing buildings for his fellow bandsmen.

The big band era ended before he lost his teeth or his hair. And at age 60, A.H. was a widower left only with his real estate business and his properties to keep him occupied—

in between annual prolonged vacations to the far corners of the globe. Last year at age 68, he married the charming widow of his lifelong best friend and travel companion.

RATING BY J.S.: A.H. has been retired all his working life—doing what he most enjoyed and doing it when he wanted to.

A perfect testimonial to my philosophy that a person should retire early, and live longer—and never retire.

CHAPTER IV

PRE-RETIREMENT FEARS

why worry -- you might not get there

The results of every study of pre-retirees has proven that their major concerns are the fear of boredom; the fear of loss of status, the fear of being physically incapacitated; the fear of the lack of financial security; loneliness; and loss of work recognition and work relationships.

Of these concerns, the three most prevalent are (1) financial (2) physical and (3) boredom.

It would be interesting to poll each reader.

How would you vote? What would be your greatest fear if you were scheduled to retire five or ten years from today?

Pre-retirement attitudes often change when the person gets closer to R day. A person 45 may be looking forward to retirement because he is bored with his nine to five job, but when he is a year away from the gold watch day, he may begin to get jittery and dread forced absence from his job. That is why planning is important. Such as Y.M. failed to do.

PROFILE OF Y.M.

Retired at age 70.

Founder and senior partner in a professional service firm.

Was looking forward to retirement since he could then play golf every day, and play bridge every evening—pastimes that he loved passionately.

Six months prior to retirement date, he suddenly began to get the heebie-jeebies and by the time R Day arrived, he and his wife were not so sure.

Why?

My theory is that both began to realize that although each had their own bridge parties, it would now become a togetherness date. She had been playing regularly with her girl friends for the fun of sharing tea and cookies, whereas he had been playing with his men friends a most serious game for a penny a point—and that is serious—much more expensive than tea and cookies.

The games where each went their separate ways were no more, now it was going to be a money bridge player with a tea and cookie partner. And that can only lead to arguments between north and south.

Add another problem. He is an avid golfer—she has never played golf—but she is willing to learn—if he will teach her.

RATING BY J.S.: Waited too long to retire and did not

make plans as to what they could both retire to.

Bridge and golf will cause such serious problems, he might
as well go back to work. (He did.)

* * * * * * * * * *

However, I am not in agreement with some professional
educators in the field of Gerontology who are so imbued
with pre-retirement planning, they advocate it for people in
their 20's and 30's. This is ridiculous.

Young people should not be concerned with aging except in relation to their parents and grandparents. Providing
for one's wife and children is involvement enough for our
youth and young middle-aged population. Young parents
have enough trouble with financial planning for the car payments, life insurance, the mortgage, Junior's orthodontist,
blue jeans, college, and a host of other expenses. When the
children are on their own, and Mom and Pop are all alone in
the three bedroom two bathroom house, they can then start
their pre-retirement planning.

There are some notable exceptions. A military man,
or a policeman who joined the force at age 21 and knows
that he is going to retire at age 41, can and should start his
planning much sooner. For when it comes to pre-retirement
planning, there is no better route to financial security than to
have 35% to 50% of your full working salary as a base at age
41, in addition to your new job earnings. This is an excellent
foundation for a comfortable financial future. I am envious.
They are by far the best careers possible for any man or
woman from a financial standpoint. And these fortunate
people, I assure you, look forward to retirement. They plan
to go back to work, and retire again.

A recent study revealed that a military officer retiring
in 1976 after 20 years of service receives a pension equal to

44% *more* than the pay he received in those decades. An enlisted man will receive 32% *more* than his pay over the same period. And he is young enough to complete a second career and obtain a second pension. However, the pension for an average civilian retiring in his 60's would total 70% to 80% *less* than what he earned in the last 20 years of his work.

If I were a policeman or in the military, I would take my early retirement BEFORE the country wakes up and severely curtails the early pension benefits. Because that day must come, for most of our public employee plans are infected with a chain-letter philosophy. They are no different than a Ponzi rip-off. No industrial profit-making company could promise so much, backed by so little.

But don't worry—our chain-letter economy will no doubt pay off on any of its commitments, even though our great grandchildren will have to cover the deficit.

Remember—the first names listed in the chain-letter get the money—and the others pay the postage.

PROFILE OF C.M.

Retired in 1976 at age 39.

C.M. grew up in a town in Texas where the major industries were oil pipe line and well drilling. His father and brothers were all so employed, but C.M. felt the work was much too dangerous—so he joined the U.S. Air Force at age 18.

During his 21 year hitch he acquired a wife who accepted the role of military wife without complaint, because she knew he would retire at an early age and they would have many years of settled down living.

C.M. progressed to the rank of Sergeant and his income (including flight pay, specialty and housing allowance) rose to $1600 monthly. However his base pay was about $800, therefore when he retired his pension was $400 (50% of base pay).

After retirement, he began an 18 month school term in order to get an aeronautical degree. The schooling entitled him to $350 a month under the G.I. Bill of Rights. At the end of the school term he will be qualified to take a job as a licensed F.A.A. maintenance supervisor, which should pay him top money.

RATING BY J.S.: Although C.M.'s income is only $750 monthly, he is a wealthy man. He has a pension which would cost about $85,000 to purchase. He and his dependents have life-time hospital and medical coverage *without premiums to pay*. He is working on airplanes—toys that he loves. And best of all, he says, "I no longer have a phone in my bedroom." (A necessity for years, since he was on call on a 24 hour basis.)

* * * * * * * * * *

Pre-retirement attitudes of the military are far different than the rest of us. In the recruitment of military, police and fire protection personnel, the generosity and short term pension program is so strongly emphasized that retirement is a pleasant prospect. Their attitude is therefore usually positive and unwavering all the way to retirement day.

The majority of the rest of us however, develop attitudes toward retirement that keep changing as R Day draws closer. When we are young, many of us look forward to retirement, anticipating the time when we will be free to "do our own thing." When middle-aged, we might dread it. As we get close to it, hopefully, we revert to our earlier attitude.

For our attitude NOW, is always influenced by our financial situation NOW (and our HOPES in relation thereto at retirement age) and/or our physical condition NOW (and our FEARS in relation thereto at retirement age).

CHAPTER V

FINANCIAL PLANNING

best to live to spend

If you cannot manage financially today on your working wage and investments, then you are my most troublesome reader. For retirement spells a smaller income and I cannot come up with any remarkably clever strategy to whisk away your fear. Telling you to start to plan, to buy insurance, to buy annuities, to buy property, are palliatives that are as useless as they are obvious.

Before inflation became accepted as a way of life, you might have agreed that you could retire and survive on an income which was substantially less than your working income. If we leave the specter of inflation out of our discussion we can still proceed on that premise. For that is a fact of life: retirement for most of us means getting along on less.

(I do not intend to ignore INFLATION—that will be dealt with, but unfortunately not disposed of, in another chapter.)

Public employees may take issue with my statement that retirement means getting along on less, for many of them are expecting as much as 75% to 100% of their highest salary as a pension. They are certainly not in the financial fear category, except that they should be aware that the city, county, state, and even federal system might one day have to face up to reality. New York City is but the first to admit its insolvency, due in large part, to the generosity-idiocy of its pension plans.

Whether or not public employees are entitled to super-fringe benefits is not the issue. The unfunded liability for what has already been promised, is.

President Carter should be commended for the passage of legislation calling for a complete reorganization of the Civil Service System. This could be the opening gun against some of our sacred cows, and no cow is more sacred than our public employee pension program. I predict that the future MUST bring about a lower level of pension benefits. And the future is NOW because of the tax revolt of 1978 spear-headed by California's Proposition 13. Today's unfunded liability will not be eradicated by a reduction in pension benefits, because the reduction will, no doubt be applicable only to newly hired public employees.

* * * * * * * * * * * * * *

The first step in pre-retirement planning for anyone is PLAY THE 65 GAME.

Make believe you are now age 65. No matter whether you are 40, 45, 50, 55, or 60, assume you are 65 TODAY. This means that you also advance the ages of your children, your savings account, your investment accruals, your mortgage. Also adjust your living expenses downward. No more expenses for children, college, etc. Less cost for clothes and entertainment. Hopefully your mortgage will be paid off, or close to it. And you can, in most instances, completely eliminate your life insurance premiums and probably reduce your hospital insurance premiums substantially (as I did).

Now list your age 65 income. How much will your company pension plan provide; Social Security; interest on projected savings accounts; income from property, etc.? If your total projected retirement income is 50% of your working days income, you should be able to get by—if 60%, you certainly should—and if 75% or more, you know you can. (Don't argue with me, Bub. I said "forget inflation." I'll talk about inflation later. I did not promise to solve it. I said I would talk about it.)

* * * * * * * * * * * * * *

Throughout your adult life, you are accustomed to paying premiums for insurance. Insurance is similar to the game of BINGO—only a few winners, but it's a game you dare not quit playing. However, since retirement means less income for most of us, let's see if we dare reduce our insurance premiums.

You probably cannot do anything about your fire, casualty, and liability premiums, but you might be able to reduce your hospital and life premium outlay considerably.

Let us take a good look at hospital insurance—the most over-rated, over-publicized, over-inflated subject of our nightmares. You dare not live to die without it.

Everyone of us will be ill for a few days or a few weeks, and the expense should be neither unexpected nor bankrupting.

Anyone of us might be seriously ill and hospitalized for an extended period, and the expense is unexpected and bankrupting.

When you read the scary insurance brochures telling you that "1 out of every 7 people will go to the hospital this year"–DON'T PANIC. Read it again. Doesn't it really say that "6 out of every 7 people will NOT go to the hospital this year?" The odds are in your favor. Insurance companies are betting YOU WON'T go to the hospital this year, nor next year nor the year after, otherwise they would not offer you a policy. So don't let fear cause you to be over-insured.

By far, the largest group that are over-insured are the Senior Citizens. They are on every insurance company's mailing list as most apt to buy. Many are paying much more for hospital insurance than they can afford. There are many instances where they do without the necessities of life to pay for five to ten hospital policies, believing the insurance will save them from the dreaded rest home. Hospital insurance will not keep them out of the rest home–paying the premiums may hasten the day they enter the home. For no policy will pay hospital costs forever, but the premiums will go on forever.

I agree that hospital insurance is essential, but not to the extent that some might lead you to believe. Don't buy insurance for the minor items. If you try to insure against every expense for every dollar from the very first dollar– you are paying too much for too little.

Let's see how this applies to the over age 65 (if you are not yet 65, read on, for you will be). You will be covered by Medicare A and B. I am not explaining the details of Medicare, for each year it must change (due to inflation, which it feeds). But it will probably always provide the major portion of medical/hospital costs, for at least a 90 day period.

What should you do about hospital insurance in addition to your Medicare? Nothing, if you cannot afford it. If you can afford to pay, you cannot afford to pay without careful study of the various plans offered. But how can the layman make the correct decision when every policy is different? Even an experienced insurance man like me found it difficult to make this decision at the time my wife and I became eligible for Medicare. I give you the results of my comparative study as a guide, so that you might better understand what to buy, or what you have bought.

My wife and I had a Major Medical policy purchased 20 years ago. It was $500 deductible/ $25 per day hospital/ up to $1000 surgery schedule/ $7500 maximum for any illness or accident. The premium was $116 a year—now it is $300 a year. (We also had group coverage while I was employed.) For the past few years, my wife has been enrolled in the American Association of Retired Persons (AARP) In-Hopital Plan at a cost of $6 monthly.

> NOTE: I am not including Blue Cross or Blue Shield in my study, because the many state and local Blues have contracts that differ in benefits and costs.

> The program sponsored and solicited by AARP has Open Enrollment periods, when everyone is accepted regardless of physical condition. This was important because of my wife's medical history. And their insurance policies are identical in benefits and costs in all states. Therefore, this is how I compared the three AARP policies offered to our group (65 and over).

MY ANALYSIS OF AARP 'IN-HOSPITAL' POLICIES

(Based on Open Enrollment brochures 2/28/77. Figures rounded off to nearest dollar.)

NOTE:
(MEDICARE provides major portion daily hospital costs for 90 days)

NO MEDICARE BENEFITS
(except one time 60 day Reserve)

AARP Policy	In-Hospital Daily Benefit	Begins	and then Daily Benefit 61st to 90 days	and then Daily Benefit 91st day to end of Benefits	Extra Benefits	Maximum Collectible per Benefit Period	Premium Monthly
Extended (1)	$10 or $14.28	1st day	$10	$ 20 to 365th day	See (a) below	$6360 plus Surgical Schedule	$8.50
In-Hospital (2)	$20	8th day	$30	$ 50 to 371st day	NONE	$16,100	$6.00
Mature Med. (3)	$30	61st day	$30	$125 to $50,000	See (b) below	$50,000 (including extra benefits (b))	$4.50

NOTE: (a) Surgery schedule up to $200. (See next page.)
(b) See next page.

You will note that Policy No. 3—the least expensive—gives much greater benefits BUT only after a 60 day period. Policy No. 1 and No. 2 begin to pay much earlier and cost more.

So No. 3 is obviously best for the serious prolonged hospital stay. BUT there are very few prolonged stays and very many short (and expensive) stays. A long stay is disastrous.

Before I made my decision, I decided to compare the amounts each policy would pay for various hospital periods: short, not so short, and prolonged.

I also compared the amounts receivable from every combination of two of the three AARP policies. Here are the results:

MY COMPARISON OF TOTAL IN-HOSPITAL BENEFITS PROVIDED BY AARP "IN-HOSPITAL" POLICIES FOR VARIOUS HOSPITALIZATION PERIODS TO MAXIMUM

	Total Received for Hospital Period of					Daily Benefit from 91st Day	Total Received		Maximum collectible per Benefit Period	Premium Monthly
	7 Days	14 Days	30 Days	60 Days	90 Days		120 Days	180 Days		
Single AARP (1)	$100*	$200	$428	$733	$1033	$20 per*	$1633*	$2833*	$6360 see (a) below	$8.50
(2)	NONE	$140	$460	$1040	$1940	$50 per	$3440	$6440	$16,100	$6.00
(3)	NONE	NONE	NONE	NONE	$900	$125 per	$4650	$12,150	$50,000 see (b) below	$4.50
Combination of Policies										
(2) & (3)	NONE	$140	$460	$1040	$2840	$175 per	$8090	$18590	$66100	$10.50
(1) & (3)	$100*	$200	$428	$733	$1933	$145 per	$6283	$14983	$56360	$13.00
(1) & (2)	$100*	$340	$888	$1733	$2933	$70 per	$5073	$9273	$22460	$14.50

NOTES: *Policy (1) figured at $14.28 per day which is amount paid (for 31 days) if surgery performed, otherwise $10 per day.

(a) Plus a surgical schedule allowing (examples) $2 for drainage of cyst to $200 for total colon resection.

(b) Policy (3) also pays 20% of reasonable fees of physician or surgeon for 1 visit a day—plus 20% reasonable surgery fee plus $20 per 8 hour shift (3 shifts a day—maximum 30 shifts) for registered nurse, etc. These extra benefits paid from 1st day of hospital stay but charged against the $50,000 total.

The author accepts no responsibility for these figures. Copy of his worksheet furnished as a guide only.

For my money, I chose the combination of No. 2 and No. 3.

So I added No. 3 to my wife's policy (she already had No. 2)—total premium $10.50 per month. And for myself, I applied for No. 2 and No. 3—another $10.50.

Then I terminated our 20 year old Major Medical. The result was that:

I gave up		Replaced it with
$500	Deductible	1st 7 days

Hospital Daily Benefits

$25 per day	1st 7 days	....	None
$25 per day	8th to 61st day	....	$20 per day
$25 per day	61st to 90th day	....	$60 per day
$25 per day	91st to maximum	....	$175 per day
$7500 for	maximum	....	$66,100 for
each of us			each of us

NOTE: I was paying $300 a year for the Major Medical plus $72 a year for my wife's AARP policy. Now instead of $372, I am paying $252, paying much less for much more.

Remember you get what you pay for. If you want early dollar coverage, you won't get long term coverage. It is your choice. My wife and I may be hospitalized for short stays and not receive one penny from our AARP policies. But some day I reasoned, one of us may be hospitalized 60/90/120/180 /365 days. I wanted the peace of mind of knowing we wouldn't be bankrupt if this happens.

WARNING: My conclusions do not mean that I am recommending AARP to the exclusion of Blue Cross, Blue Shield, or other insurance company plans. Preceding figures and comparisons are given to show how one may compare

policies. In 1979, the AARP sponsored group health insurance programs no longer offered the policies that I referred
to as (1) and (3), but instead began an aggressive solicitation
for more expensive policies with major emphasis on first day
hospital benefits.

* * * * * * * * * * * * * *

Now, what to do about life insurance?

My involvement in the life insurance business leaves me
believing that just about everyone has purchased life insurance to protect someone he loves. I also believe that as we
approach retirement, many of us continue to pay the premiums even though it may be a burden on a retirement income. I feel that the majority don't know what they can do
with their policies.

So, many continue to pay the premiums, and if the
premiums are no financial burden, fine. But if paying causes
money problems, then it is not so fine. Many others cash in
their policies and worry because they no longer have insurance protection. If they needed the cash or have no beneficiary, well and good. Otherwise this may not be a smart
move. And then there are those who stop paying premiums
and drop the policies. This is the most self-defeating choice
of all, because most policies, if over three years in force are
not dropped, for they do have value that could continue
the insurance protection *in full force* for a number of years.

So if you would like to learn all you should know about
life insurance, read on. You may be pleasantly surprised to
learn that your dropped life policies may have valuable
options, appropriately called NON-FORFEITURE VALUES,
values that you do not lose, providing you with options from
which to choose. (Not applicable to most "term" policies.)

Following is a reproduction of two pages of a life insurance company agent's instructional manual. This was

written by this author over 20 years ago (in a novel attempt
to present non-forfeiture values, stripped of legalistic actuarial language so that it could be better understood by the
non-insurance-agent reader.)

NON-FORFEITURE VALUES

Non-forfeiture values mean that there are values in your policy that
you do not forfeit even though you discontinue paying premiums
prior to the end of the contract period.

Usually there are no values for the first two or three years of a
policy. The non-forfeiture values are (1) cash surrender or loan value
(2) paid-up insurance (3) extended term insurance. (There are usually no non-forfeiture values on 5 Year Term, 10 Year Term, Family
Income or Mortgage Protection.)

(1) CASH SURRENDER VALUE—This is the amount of money
that you may receive if you wish to cash in your policy. The cash
values are smaller for whole life policies and much larger for endowment plans because premiums are likewise. (Same amount as the
Loan Value.)

LOAN VALUE—The insured may borrow on any policy any
amount up to the cash surrender value by paying interest at the rate
of 5%. *Older policies only—higher rates on new policies.* There is
no time limit on repayment of the loan and the policy continues in
full effect by the payment of premiums and interest, excepting that
it has a loan against it. In the event of death, the loan would be de-
ducted from the face amount.

(2) PAID-UP INSURANCE—This is one of the most interesting of
the non-forfeiture values. Actually there is no policy (not even a
whole life) that forces the policyholder to continue payments for
any particular period. To complete your policy program you should
continue the required premiums but if you do not wish to, or circumstances make it impossible for you to do so, you may stop paying and have a paid-up policy, which *is actually a miniature* of the
identical policy that you originally purchased.

For Example: If you purchased a Whole Life policy you could have
a smaller Whole Life paid-up policy. If you purchased a 20 Year
Endowment and stopped paying after 5 years, you have a PAID-
UP 20 Year Endowment maturing 15 years later for a reduced
amount. (Should death occur, the same paid-up amount is immediately payable to the beneficiary). This feature enables a person to
continue to have some insurance on a reduced basis, even though
he stops paying his premiums prematurely.

(3) EXTENDED TERM INSURANCE—The *full* amount of insurance is continued for a definite period of time without further premium payments (acts as a paid-up term policy).

Under this option, it should be noted that under no circumstances would the extended insurance extend beyond the period of the original policy.

For Example: On a 20 Year Endowment, the extended insurance period when added to the years the policy was in force will not go beyond the 20th anniversary of the policy.

Since the extended insurance might have (except for this restriction) provided many more years insurance protection, the excess is paid in cash to the Insured at the end of the 20th year.

EXAMPLES OF THREE INSUREDS: A, B and C

All were age 40 when each purchased a $1000 (but different form of) policy.
All paid premiums for 10 years and then chose the extended insurance option.

Type of) Policy:)	A *Ordinary Life	B 20 Pay Life	C 20 Yr. End't.
Extended) Insurance)	11 Years & 282 Days	17 Years & 113 Days	10 Years & then $428 Cash.

Note: A person is entitled to only one of the foregoing three options at any one time. If no selection is made and premiums are discontinued, the policy will automatically go on extended insurance if it has values at that time. (This company's rule—check your policy—it might differ.)

*Ordinary Life also called Straight Life, Whole Life, Life Paid Up at Age 85 or Life Paid Up at Age 96.

Therefore, you can discontinue paying premiums and have a paid-up policy for a lesser amount, or you can have the *same* amount of insurance for a definite *period of time* (or you can turn in the policy for its cash value).

I will show you exactly what I did and why.

When I quit my full-time salaried position, I had to reduce my expenses and since my life insurance premiums amounted to a sizable figure, this was a good place to begin. My goal was to discontinue paying any more premiums—but my problem was that I still wanted some insurance to be payable to my wife upon my death.

Let's look at just one of my policies and I will show you what I did, why I did it, and what doing it did for me and my wife.

EXAMPLE: $20,000 Whole Life, 18½ years in force, and it had the following non-forfeiture values: (Figures rounded off for clarity—$11,000 was $10,980, etc.) Annual premium was $612.

CASH (or LOAN)
$8000

PAID-UP INSURANCE
$11,000

EXTENDED TERM for
8½ years

If I were in poor health or terminally ill I would have chosen the Extended Term, since I would have known that I could not survive the 8½ year period—and the full $20,000 would have been paid to my wife *even though I paid no premiums* (provided I died before the end of the 8½ years).

Since I was in good health, I chose the $11,000 paid-up. It will be paid whenever I die, *even though I paid no more premiums.* Therefore, every year I can put the $612 premium *in my bank account.* If I live another 10 years—$6120 in the bank (plus interest).

So, (after choosing the same option on all my policies) my wife has a sizable *paid-up* insurance estate, and we have a very substantial reduction in expenses (and every year I live, I can increase our savings accounts by the annual premiums I *do not pay*).

* * * * * * * * * * * * * *

I must emphasize that what I did is not necessarily what you should do. It depends on your circumstances and goals. I wanted to increase my retirement income—which I did by reducing my retirement outgo. If your life insurance premiums total, for example, $5000 annually, and you place your policies on the paid-up option—you have $5000 more each year to use for retirement living. But it is essential that this leaves you enough paid-up life insurance for the needs of your spouse and estate.

And if your insurance is participating (pays you annual dividends) your $5000 premiums may cost you only $2000 after deducting the annual dividends—so old policies that are earning substantial dividends are best to continue on a premium-paying basis.

When you are studying the advisability of discontinuing your life insurance premiums, you must be sure to check your non-forfeiture values (which are clearly shown in your policies) with your agent (verified by a letter from the company) and make your choice based upon your own needs and *especially* your physical condition.

* * * * * * * * * * * * * *

NOTE 1. To members of family of a terminally ill *insured.*

When an insured person is terminally ill, his life insurance premiums are always continued by his family even though it might be a serious financial burden.
The family should check the Extended Term Option. If the Extended Term is 10 years, and the doctor says the insured has only one or two years expectancy—why pay any more premiums?
BUT make certain the Extended Term goes into effect. Many policies state that if premiums are not paid, then Extended Term is automatic—many other policies will require the signature of the insured for the selection.
Check with the company. This is not a gimmick. This is legitimate.

NOTE 2.

If you wish to continue paying premiums, but you could use or need a little extra money—and *if you have an old policy which charges only 5% interest on loans*—(and most oldies do)—borrow the full cash value and invest in a long term certificate in your savings and loan association, paying you at least 7½%. Continue to pay your premium *plus* the 5% interest (interest is tax deductible) and receive 7½% from the S. & L. (taxable).

EXAMPLE: My $20,000 policy (on previous page) had a loan value of $8000.

I could have borrowed $8000 and deposited it in a 6 Year Certificate and collected 7½% or $600 each year, and paid the insurance company 5%, or $400 each year (plus the regular premium).

In event of insured's death, policy pays $20,000 less $8000 loan—but the $8000 is not lost because you have an $8000 Certificate.

Also not a gimmick—perfectly legit.

P.S.: Please do not make a loan against a policy to lend to brother-in-law, even if he promises to pay 10%.

CHAPTER VI

NO ONE NEED FEAR BOREDOM

when someone needs someone

*Boredom (and loneliness) is the third most popular of the pre-retiree fears. It is real to some, half-imagined by others, and really imagined by most. Even those who have always led a boring and lonely life, will find that constructive retirement can be an antidote to boredom and loneliness. For on retiring, one establishes a new and wonderful bond, a common kinship with other retirees. All it takes to bring loneliness and boredom to an end is to bring two lonely people together, unless both are bores, in which case they are still better off because misery likes company.

My use of the term *imagined* is deliberate, since I con-

*No, I did not forget that PHYSICAL is the No. 2 most worrisome fear. That, like INFLATION will be dealt with in a later chapter.

tend that loneliness is not a legitimate fear. It is an over-used abused excuse for inactivity. No man or woman who is physically and mentally alert need ever fear or experience continuing boredom or loneliness. You are invited to join a vast army of 37 million volunteers who turn in some of their bored and lonely hours for productive useful companion-able hours. Hundreds of programs under federal, state, county, and city sponsorship have a continuing need for vol-unteer help—I will touch upon only a few.

The federal agency called ACTION has a purpose that cannot be criticised by anyone, no matter what his philoso-phy or political belief. Those who are familiar with ACTION agree that the world would truly be a better place in which to live if this agency's aims and teachings could be spread throughout all nations. In fact it is, through one of its pro-grams, The Peace Corps. The Peace Corps has American volunteers working in 68 countries, invited by the host gov-ernment, to provide training and technical assistance. There is no age limit and over 7000 adventuresome *retirees* have represented The Peace Corps in all parts of the world.

Among ACTION's domestic programs are a number that are geared to the older age volunteer, such as
    Foster Grandparents (FGP)
    Senior Companion Programs (SCP)
    Retired Senior Volunteer Program (RSVP)
    Volunteers in Service to America (VISTA).

Foster Grandparents (FGP) is, as its name implies, a program to serve children who have special needs. Each grandparent is assigned two children and he or she devotes two hours a day (5 days a week) to each child on a person-to-person basis. The setting may be a correctional or mental institution, or a home for handicapped, emotionally dis-turbed, dependent or neglected children. It might also be a school, day care center, or even in the child's own home.

To become a Foster Grandparent, one must be 60 or older, have a low income, and be of good health.

The FGP receives a modest hourly stipend, transportation or travel allowance, hot lunches where available, annual physical exam, and accident insurance.

* * * * * * * * * * * * * *

The Senior Companions Programs (SCP) serves adults who have special needs. The setting could be a nursing home, institution, or even the adult's home.

The volunteers are also recruited from the lower income older person group, so that the daily stipend and other direct benefits might also serve to provide the volunteer with financial assistance. So both the volunteer and the person being served are benefited by this program. However, the main objective is to enable older persons to remain in their own homes.

* * * * * * * * * * * * *

The Retired Senior Volunteer Program (RSVP) is an all encompassing community project. This is open to all age 60 or over, regardless of income. It pays nothing except reimbursement of expenses, such as travel, lunch—but it pays a great deal in that it provides purpose and a meaningful life for those who have a need to be needed.

RSVP serves public or private non-profit organizations such as hospitals, nursing homes, libraries, schools. No matter what a person's skill or experience, he or she is needed as an RSVP. RSVP's slogan "to make life a little better for someone else and yourself" says it all.

* * * * * * * * * * * * *

Volunteers In Service To America (VISTA) is not limited to older age volunteers. I include it for those retirees who desire full-time involvement in poverty-related community needs. This program requires a minimum of one year full-time service, living and working in the low income community. It provides nominal salaries and allowances.

* * * * * * * * * * * * * *

In addition to, and in cooperation with ACTION is a private, non-profit organization called The NATIONAL CENTER FOR VOLUNTARY ACTION (NCVA). Its primary purpose is to assist community organizations to recruit volunteers by providing greater recognition, utilization, and coordination of volunteers.

NCVA operates at the local level through over 300 affiliated Voluntary Action Centers (VAC) throughout the country.

In addition to volunteerism without pay, the VAC's through their extensive community activities, can also direct the pre-retiree or older person to job-for-pay opportunities. It supports and directs many local non-profit programs whose efforts are in the same area. For example, The Second Careers Program.

* * * * * * * * * * * * * *

The Second Careers Program is basically funded by a grant from the Edna McConnell Clark Foundation of New York. The Los Angeles Voluntary Action Center was named to act as fiscal agent for this pilot program in Southern California to direct, recognize, and utilize the substantial productive potential of older persons.

Second Careers recognizes the problems of an *ever-increasing,* healthier, better trained, more qualified, *but non-*

productive group—and an *ever-decreasing* active work force. By the year 2000, it is expected that over one-third of the U.S. population will be retired. This program calls upon employers to conserve the production of older age persons in part-time, temporary, or full time jobs. They work closely with management and personnel departments and foster pre-retirement planning for the company's own employees, with emphasis on "second careers" both in paid assignments and in voluntary community projects without pay.

It is expected that Second Careers will become nationwide as it gains support and funding from more and more participating employer companies.

Obviously, this author enthusiastically endorses the Second Careers Program, since its purpose coincides with the theme of this book.

Although M.G. never heard of this program, he certainly planned well for his second career.

PROFILE OF M.G.

Retired at age 60, as planned since 50.

M.G. was a school teacher for over 30 years. He taught printing, but he hated printing because he said it robbed him of the chance to prove that he was ever capable of doing anything else. The public, and even his fellow teachers, did not seem to consider printing as an educational course. He felt as though he were low man on the totem pole. He was determined that he would someday become successful in another field, far removed from printing.

At age 50, M.G. had decided on the new venture—real estate. He could test it on a part-time basis and still maintain his teaching duties until he could retire at age 60 from the school system.

He was rejected by the real estate firms—they said it was because no one could sell houses working only evenings and weekends. But perhaps it was because M.G. was a most unlikely looking salesman—too short, too fat, too unimpressive, and he stammered. But he was so persistent that he finally wore one firm down so that they agreed to take him on. He studied, took the exam, and passed for his license. Weeks went by, and M.G. was the best meeting attendee and the most non-productive salesman in the agency. After five months, he told the manager that he was now confident that he knew enough to start selling. This was the joke of the week.

The end of the first year as a part-time real estate salesman, found M.G. No. 10 in the 45 man agency. The second year he was No. 1—and for the next eight years, he was never lower than No. 3. By the time he retired from teaching, his income from real estate was five times his teaching salary. And M.G. now needed a C.P.A. to do his tax returns.

At age 60, he became a full time salesman (he refused the manager's spot) and he has been No. 1 ever since.

RATING BY J.S.: Everyone has dreams of achieving certain goals. A few do something about it.

Pre-retirement planning is an individual problem that can only be solved by that individual.

If M.G. had asked my advice (before 50) I would no doubt have suggested that he open his own print shop to retire to. But he had the courage and determination to discard the obvious and tackle the impossible. In addition to monetary gains beyond his expectations, M.G. no longer is too short or too fat. He is now very impressive and no longer stammers.

* * * * * * * * * * * * * *

No one willing and able to work, can find a more receptive ear than NCVA or its specialized affiliate organizations. It has a list of over 2000 volunteer job categories, and although NCVA cannot be expected to have openings in every category and in every locality, the retiree (whether a typist, a lion tamer, a blackjack dealer, or an executive) would do well to check this agency out.

Many persons who have been out of the job market, have found that volunteer work is an excellent method of testing and developing new skills, or learning a new occupation. As an example, take a displaced homemaker who has just completed a typing or secretarial study course. If she accepts a volunteer assignment, she can become proficient and gain the confidence she needs to take her place in the job-for-pay market.

* * * * * * * * * * * * * *

And let's not forget the vast non-profit community activities such as your church, hospital, USO, Red Cross, United Way, Goodwill, Salvation Army, City of Hope, etc. Such groups play important national and community roles. And without the input of millions of concerned, unselfish, and productive volunteers, they could not exist.

You and I know so many volunteers, that it is difficult to select only one to profile. I believe T.M. is typical of all who give support and sustenance to others.

PROFILE OF T.M.

Retired at age 60.

T.M. was a school teacher, superintendent, and a teachers' teacher in a private school system. She lived prudently in order to travel extravagantly. Every few years she would go to a foreign country, and live with a native family all summer vacation, so that she could observe the customs and speak the language. Once she was so enamored that she stayed on for two years, and taught English in that country's public schools.

She looked forward to retirement in order to change her career, and as she says it, "To have the freedom to do or not to do—and set the alarm clock only when I wanted to."

Since retirement she has been working as a volunteer for the blind. She has been proofreading for foreign language transcriptions in Braille—so she is studying Braille.

She always loved to play piano but never had the time to practice. Now she has the time to take piano lessons and to practice.

I imagine her next trip will be to Japan. But not as most American tourists, for she will speak the language fluently, since she is studying Japanese in her spare time.

RATING BY J.S.: T.M. has not retired from teaching—she has merely changed classrooms.

She has an insatiable drive for knowledge. Although she is involved in Senior Citizen causes, she questions the time and money spent by churches, city, and federal agencies on group activities for retirees.

"Retirees who can participate in senior socials, sports and group cross country trips, should also consider giving a few hours of their time to visiting the sick and disabled who cannot. I would like to see that added to the list of group activities." That's what she says—and I agree.

* * * * * * * * * * * * * *

CHAPTER VII

COLLECT SOCIAL SECURITY

no need to wait for your brother

I advocate retiring BEFORE not AFTER, EARLY not LATE.

I am not proposing that everyone retire at age 40, although policemen, firemen, and military can and should. I wish they had more incentive to remain on the job, but when a man can get 35% to 50% of his full salary at the end of 20 years (he often reasons that if he continues on the job, he is only receiving 50% to 65% of his salary), he has every incentive to quit, and I would too.

Since L.C. also could retire after 25 years, he did.

PROFILE OF L.C.

Retired at 55, two years ago.

After 25 years as an electrical engineer with one of the major aircraft plants, L.C. quit at 55 on his company pension.

His wife has an excellent position and is continuing to work until she is 60. Her company does not allow retirement until age 60, otherwise she too would be now listed as a retiree.

L.C. has accepted a two day a week assignment with an electronics firm but doesn't punch the clock. He chooses his own hours to work and even the days.

He gets up each morning at the usual time, and as before, he drives his wife to work and picks her up at 5 P.M. Nothing has changed since his retirement—not even his income. For his pension plus his two day a week gives him the same income as his previous full salary. But now he can go fishing in the middle of the week and spend enjoyable hours working at rehabilitating their motor home.

RATING BY J.S.: L.C. and wife are as content as before retirement and they will be a happy retired couple after Mrs. L.C. retires.

They prepared and planned their retirement precisely and look forward to each phase. They are a model couple, who truly will make retirement "the best years of their lives."

* * * * * * * * * *

For the large segment whose major pension is Social Security, there is also an incentive to retire at age 62, instead of waiting until 65.

However, Social Security will not provide the luxuries of life, so if you haven't accumulated enough assets by 62—you have a problem. But you are going to have the same problem three years hence, so why not face it now?

There are many who do not have the guts to face it now, or at 62, or at 65. It is my hope that some may be comforted by this writing to gain enough courage to do voluntarily, and at a moment of their choice, that, which most will be forced to do on their 65th birthday. (The passage of the law in 1978 changing mandatory retirement from age 65, to age 70, doesn't change my recommendation to retire early. Nor will it change the trend to retire earlier, rather than later.)

And let's clear up once and for all time this old-age syndrome. Quit blaming your spouse, the government, your boss, or the system as you near retirement. The young are at your heels, and that is as it should be. It is a natural evolution that older people turn over their positions to younger people. You thought it was O.K. when you were climbing the ladder.

No one need feel sorry for the senior citizens. We have all been senior citizens since age 50, according to . . . who? who did start classifying the middle-aged, as oldsters? And who started the rumor that they are all underprivileged?

I feel sorry for the older people who are poor, sickly, or disabled, and especially for those who are alone. BUT I also feel sorry for the *young* people who are poor, sickly, disabled, and alone. It is *poor, sickly, disabled, alone*—those conditions deserve our empathy—*age* does not merit sympathy.

It is time to recognize the truth. Senior citizens as a group, have more wealth than any other age group—by far. There is no question but that our older citizens own most of the property, stocks, bonds, and savings bank accounts in the country. A survey by the U.S. Savings and Loan League, showed that almost 70% of the savings accounts of over $5000, were held by people over age 55. That's no surprise, is it? You can't expect the young to own much, and the middle-aged haven't had as many years as the seniors, to accumulate as much. And if you split the seniors into the two major sexes (am I allowed by law to differentiate?) you will find, that the female segment owns and controls, probably 75% or more of this enormous wealth. (Which is epitomized by a recent happening on a TV talk show. The subject was Women's Lib, and one woman astonished the other women on the panel, when she said she was *against* Women's Lib. When asked "Why?" she said, "I'm not for giving the men 50%. We women have 75% now.")

So let's not think of older folks as necessarily poor. Some are—*but a smaller percentage than in any other age group.*

But, whether rich or poor, age 62 or 65 is a Social Security decision-making time for most everyone, and everyone should give serious consideration to retiring earlier, in stead of later (S.S. wise).

Why? Because at age 62, a man or woman can receive 80% of the Social Security pension he, or she, would receive at age 65. Don't forget my warning of signs that the rules governing this chain-letter may be changed.

The person who is staying at his job until he reaches 65 only because of his Social Security pension is, in my opinion, making a mistake money-wise, for the guy who retires at 62 will be ahead of the 65 retiree until the age of 78. After age 78, the 65 retiree will begin to pass the 62 in dollars received. I think the chances of living 16 years after 62 are much better than after age 78. Does anyone disagree?

To illustrate this point, let us assume you have a twin

brother. You decide to retire at age 62 and take 80% pension (assume $80 for simplicity). Your brother decides to go on until 65 so he can receive $100 a month. This is how it works out.

By Age	$80 x 12		$100 x 12		Whose ahead? How much?
	You have collected		Your brother collected		
	During Year	Total since 62	During year	Total since 65	
63	$960	$ 960	− 0 −		You + $960
64	960	1920	− 0 −		You + $1920
65	960	2880	− 0 −		You + $2880
66	960	3840	$1200	$ 1200	You + $2640
67	960	4800	1200	2400	You + $2400
68	960	5760	1200	3600	You + $2160
69	960	6720	1200	4800	You + $1920
70	960	7680	1200	6000	You + $1680
71	960	8640	1200	7200	You + $1440
72	960	9600	1200	8400	You + $1200
73	960	10560	1200	9600	You + $960
74	960	11520	1200	10800	You + $720
75	960	12480	1200	12000	You + $480
76	960	13440	1200	13200	You + $220
77	960	14440	1200	14400	EQUAL
78	960	15360	1200	15640	Brother + $240
79	960	16320	1200	16800	Brother + $480
80	960	17280	1200	18000	Brother + $720

NOTE: These comparative figures do not take into consideration S.S. cost of living increases.

Until 1978, early retirees received the same increases as those who retired at age 65, but beginning in 1979, all early retirees will receive reduced increases. Therefore, although one may still retire at 62 on an 80% (of age 65) pension, because of the new formula relating to increases, the age 65 retiree (in the preceding example) may pass the age 62 retiree, at age 76 or 75.

I still recommend early retirement, but it is obvious that our political fathers would rather you didn't. So in 1978 they slipped in another early retiree penalty—the early retiree cannot *earn* as much as the 65 retiree before losing some of his benefits.

So changes are on the way, as I have been predicting for many years.

Let's not forget your employer's pension plan. The same early retirement formula should be applicable, as the actuarial assumptions should be closely similar. So consider also the merits of taking an 80% company pension starting at 62, instead of 100% at 65. It should show the early bird ahead until age 78, same as the Social Security example.

NOTE: Some pension plans do not allow receiving pensions at an earlier age but will defer the payments until you reach 65, even though you retired at 62. But I don't know a single plan that would not permit early retirement pension payments in event of disability, and they are usually most lenient in their interpretation of disability.

So why wait? IF YOU CAN AFFORD TO RETIRE AT 65, CAN YOU AFFORD TO WAIT UNTIL 65?

P.S.: Someone in the balcony is sure to shout, "You're forgetting that the man who quits at 62 is losing his full salary for three years. Did you take that into consideration?"

Yes, I did. He is not losing three years salary. He is only losing the difference between his full salary and his pension income; his Social Security income; and his wife's Social Security income (which she too can begin to receive at 62).

I am aware that this prescription is not applicable to many of my readers. But tests prove that some readers to whom this might apply beneficially, are not aware of it.

Don't misquote me. I never said you won't get paid your Social Security benefits for the rest of your life. You will, as long as there are printing presses.

NOTE FOR EXECUTIVES: A phase-out salary plan applicable especially to management and top executives who opt for early retirement, is described in Chapter IX.

CHAPTER VIII

LOOK FORWARD TO RETIREMENT OR DREAD IT

but find out why

You love or you hate, so you are happily looking forward to retirement.

You are in love with some thing, some place, somebody; maybe your motor home, Florida, or your wife. You are a fortunate person because you have plans.

Or you hate some thing, some place, somebody; your job, Florida, or your wife. You are an unfortunate person, and you better start making plans.

And though many of you thoroughly enjoy your daily work, you are anxiously awaiting the day when you can lock up your desk for the last time. Your home life is pleasant and satisfying. Your spouse is a pleasure to come home to after a hard day at the office, even though she too has had a hard day at her office. Each respects the other's contribution and listens to the other's daily successes and failures. An ideal setting for an amiable life after retirement from a before 9 A.M. and after 5 P.M. existence. The camper in the driveway. or the boat at the Marina, or the golf clubs in the car trunk, or the fishing rod in the garage—any of these weekend vacation possessions give promise of a living happily ever after.

Sport fantasyites are fortunate folks who lose themselves in their sport hobbies. The Wednesday afternoon and Sunday morning golfer—the weekend fishing buff—the boater —the skier. All of your life you have enjoyed those fantastic hours and retirement sounds heavenly.

Please continue to look forward to retirement no matter what I say. But there are only a very few of you who will continue to enjoy the leisure activities enough to play golf or fish every day for 30% of your lifetime. What was great fun and playing hookey from your business, suddenly becomes a daily bore and no fun, and you too, will soon begin to seek a change from your long anticipated fun activities. And your home life is suddenly full time instead of part time. From this date forward you and your spouse are going to live together all day, every day, and every night. And the fun of having fun is no longer fun when you can do it at any moment, all day long, whether it is fishing, golf, or sex. And even *your* wife may revert to the old hackneyed adage, "I married you for better or worse, but not for lunch every day."

But B.R. is home for lunch every day and it's fine with Mrs. B.R.

PROFILE OF B.R.

Retired at age 65 just as prescribed by society.
His wife told me that B.R. had a lifelong ambition to retire
in order to buy a mountain cabin where he could fish, fish,
and fish. His children knew that when they were on their
own, Pop would be found relaxing on top of his mountain.

B.R. worked and saved all his life. He was a painter and as
his boys grew to manhood, he became a painting contractor, and put them all to work (including his sons-in-law).
He built a sizable business and all his family shared in its
success.

On the day he reached 65 he quit and gave the business to
his kids. His savings plus Social Security was more than
ample, and he could pay cash for the mountain cabin of his
choice.

For three months he loafed and pored through the "cabins,
For Sale" ads. But he never went out to see a single cabin,
nor did he go fishing. Now that he could any time he
wished—he didn't wish. As he explained it, "Fishing was
fun as a once in a while, but as a 'for the rest of my life'
activity, it scares the heck out of me."

So he started as a painting contractor all over again. He
would not handle any of his old customers that he had
turned over to his family. And within two years, he built
another sizable business with his wife as a partner, secretary and bookkeeper. He told me, in front of his beaming
wife, that she was the best damn office manager he had ever
had.

RATING BY J.S.: Obviously this is a successful retirement especially because both husband and wife are totally
involved.

The moment he stopped his work and was able to pursue
his beloved hobby, he discovered it was his work he loved,
and his hobby he endured.

* * * * * * * * * * * * * *

So after a long enough retiring period to get the longed-for sports out of your system, you too will take on some work for money, or if money is not important, you will become a $1 a year man assisting your church, hospital, Boy Scouts, small business, community or minority boot-strap group who sorely need and deeply appreciate your mature judgment and business expertise. And your golfing, fishing, and home life will be more fun and satisfying when they are once again part of, but not the "hole" of your life.

I feel sorry for those who opt for retirement but who have no plans as to what they are going to do with their new found freedom. Freedom to do—what? Visiting relatives back East or traveling abroad is only a vacation filler. If vacationing all the rest of your life is to your liking—fine—please enjoy. But for most of us, it just ain't enough.

If you want—plan. A college professor was not happy because he hated the brutal winters in his home town. He was a sun worshipper, a tennis enthusiast, a swimming and physical exercise nut, so he obviously looked forward to moving to a southern locale. But he enjoyed teaching so much that he tolerated his otherwise intolerable life, and as he kept getting closer to 65, he happily crossed off each passing year.

Money was not his problem. He felt he could not be completely happy in a tropical clime unless he could continue teaching. So five years before retiring, he put his plan into action. He solicited a number of colleges in warmer climates and secured assignments as a visiting professor during summer school sessions. After three such temporary part-time stints, he was able to arrange, *two years before* he retired, a full time teaching position to begin as soon as he retired.

* * * * * * * * * * * * * *

And E.C. also wants to retire for many "miniature" reasons.

PROFILE OF E.C.

In his 50's—not yet retired but anxious to.

E.C. is holding down two jobs—one for money so that he can afford to work for no money at his second job. To understand why, you must know something about the childhood of this 6 foot 3, 240 pound man.

When E.C. was six years old, he was not allowed on the merry-go-round at the town park because he was too heavy for the wooden horses. When he was nine, he was 5 feet 4½ inches tall and weighed 140 pounds. When his father tried to enroll him into the Cub Scouts, he was rejected as too big, and the Boy Scouts turned him down because he was too young. Although E.C. was a healthy lad, he was also a crippled child.

He impatiently waited to reach the age of majority so that his size and his age might be balanced and accepted without "Ain't it too bad?" by society.

Since adulthood, he has given much of his time and meager resources working and playing with crippled and disadvantaged children. For 30 years he has been avidly collecting miniature toys and he now has a collection of over 3000 which he shows at children's hospitals. His ambition is to take early retirement and to perfect his toy collection show so that he may spend full time as a big brother to his kids.

RATING BY J.S.: E.C. was not embittered by his childhood experiences but is determined that no one else suffer as he did.

Many will say that this man is merely attempting to relive his childhood. If so—the kids whose lives he touches, are fortunate, indeed.

* * * * * * * * * * * * * * *

A person's home life can affect the manner in which he views his approaching retirement. Many dreaders have a monotonous lifeless home life—a regimented life sentence in a jail (called a house), with a keeper (called a husband or wife), with fellow inmates serving much shorter sentences (called children). But home life is not entirely to blame, for many other dreaders have a happy fulfilling home life.

I believe that most people who dread retirement don't know "WHY," or if they do, they won't admit it. The answer to "WHY" is that they are worried about their loss of status as a useful, productive individual. And I mean STATUS—because work, whether as a grave digger or a top executive, is the most satisfying builder-upper for any person's ego. Even though a person may hate his job, having a job is prestigious and an unspoken proclamation that "I AM A SOMEBODY. I AM PRODUCTIVE." His paycheck was his status ticket at home. Dinner always awaited the bread-winner when he got home from work. Soon *he* will no longer be king. He might even have to get his own dinner, or eat at five (her time) instead of at his time. Yes, I maintain, it's just that simple—and complicated.

Oftentimes, the higher the executive position, the more devastating the dread of retirement. Industry has a gimmick called Chairman of the Board—a job? to which they can retire a President, at full pay, with nothing to do (I know—I was one)—otherwise they would never get him out of the president's chair.

So it is no surprise that top executive G.H. found it difficult to cope with his first *forced* retirement.

PROFILE OF G.H.

Retired at age 67—unwillingly *this* seventh time.
This man's talents are unbelievable. He has worked successfully in so many fields that his resume reads as though
he were triplets. Teacher, author, playwright, advertising,
public relations, sales executive, and nationally known lec-
turer. Never unemployed, but always besieged by better
offers in exciting new fields—so he quit. He never could
imagine that anyone might ever *ask him* to quit.

His wife is also a talented person who gave up a promising
career to inspire and bask in the light of her husband's
achievements. Mrs. G.H. has been looking forward to Mr.
G.H.'s retirement.

When G.H. reached 65 (mandatory retirement) he was not
ready. He actually had no plans and he dreaded retirement
more than any man I have ever known. He had no financial
or physical problems, but he had a mental block. His wife
pleaded with him to retire to a well earned life of leisure,
togetherness, and to write the book he never had time to
write. Instead, he got a two year extension, during which he
was to phase out and pass on his executive duties to others,
and he promised his wife, he would then retire willingly.
But he was too busy to let go, and at age 67, he was in no
better frame of mind than he was at 65. Protestingly, he
accepted his gold watch and pension.

RATING BY J.S.: At the moment of this writing, G.H. is
still an unhappy man. He has retired six or seven times before, and he does not realize it. For if retirement is a change
of work to that which one might enjoy more—he has done
so many times successfully.

I predict he will soon find another challenge that will once
again make use of his talents and he will be thoroughly en-
grossed and happily retired —but not so, for Mrs. G.H. For
Mrs. G.H. must realize that it takes two to tango, and her
man doesn't want to dance. He will always want to be the
leader of the orchestra.

CHAPTER IX

EXECUTIVES RETIRE, TOO

sooner or later

An executive is considered an indispensable man in an organization. Any business that knows its business begins to groom someone to take over an about to retire executive's duties (and salary). The question is, "When is the groom to begin to take over the old man's duties?" And what a shock it is to the vibrant, vigorous 61 year old vice president the first time he overhears someone refer to him as the Old Man.

The next shock is when the president suggests that the young taking-over groom attend the industry convention in Hawaii because the old man is needed urgently at the Home Office. How does the veep explain this to his wife, who has each year accompanied her executive husband on the annual first-class week-long, all expenses paid, convention vacation? She has already bought a new dress for the last night's formal dinner dance.

So the old man stops off at the bar before going home and bolstered by a couple of stiff drinks, he greets his wife with "Why the nerve of that little bastard! I picked him as my assistant, taught him everything he knows, and now he can't wait until I retire. The nervy pushy punk. Just wait until he gets in over his head again and asks the old man to bail him out. Just wait!"

And suddenly revenge becomes an exciting titillating thought. What better revenge than to quit? Every indispensable executive considers quitting the first time he gets the message that he is not indispensable. And that suddenly brings him (and his wife) to the reality of retirement, pension, financial status, and, more important: What is he to do with his new found free time? And after the shock waves have subsided, the first consoling irritating remark by his wife, "I wouldn't quit. That's just what they want you to do. You stay there and draw your salary until 65 even though you do nothing. You're entitled to it. You built the company!"

Now you and you alone are faced with a decision concerning ego, pride, economics, but more important your physical and mental condition for the rest of your life. Do you stay until the end and get the gold watch, or do you quit and gain more time to go to work doing that which you would most enjoy doing? And if you don't know now what that work might be—what will it be at age 65?

Are you one of the large number of executives who have no idea what your company pension plan will pay you at age 61? You fellows hesitate to ask for early retirement figures, because the chief might misunderstand and suspect that you might be contemplating quitting before the putting out to pasture day. If so, I'll tell you how to do it. Just say that your accountant wants the figures because he is reviewing your estate for tax purposes.

And suppose your salary is $60,000 a year (don't tell me I am using an unusually high figure—the U.S. President's wife has a secretary whose salary is close to $50,000), and let's assume your vested pension as of 61 would be $20,000 a year. Let's agree you would like to retire now but you hate to lose $40,000 for the next four years. How about getting someone *you can trust* to suggest to the president (of your company) that you might like to retire now, but since your pension is only $20,000, it would be nice if you were paid $40,000 for four days a week for the first year; $35,000 for three days a week the second year; $30,000 for two days a week the third year; and $25,000 for one day a week the fourth year. You would be able to phase out your duties and your salary gradually—and the company could save $130,000 over the same four year period.

This type of phase-out salary continuance has been used many times to everyone's advantage (no, you don't get your Social Security until the end of the four year period—so what?). And if you do not get a four year phase-out, but instead are invited to quit right now on your $20,000—don't sue me. Remember, it wasn't your idea—it was your trusted colleague's suggestion.

If you don't like the above idea, here is another one. Send your chief a copy of this book and inscribe on the inside of the front cover

Dear President see Page 81 for a GOOD idea

Signed Guess Who?

* * * * * * * * * * * * * *

Actually, unhappy status-conscious retiring executives
are the easiest group to prescribe for. All they need do, is
spend $10 for calling cards containing the new imposing
title "CONSULTANT."

I did it, so I know whereof I speak. Since I had been a
life insurance company executive, my new cards read
JOSEPH SCHWARTZ
CONSULTANT TO LIFE INSURANCE COMPANIES

Although I was not kept busy every day, I was able to
command a very respectable fee whenever I was called upon.
And it was satisfying. No, that's a lie because it wasn't satisfying in most assignments. Although the money was good,
the work was disillusioning. For most often, I was engaged
by small unprofitable companies who were desperately cop-
ing with a real problem. Usually the problem was the President who had hired me to solve the problem. So I would suggest a private meeting (just the two of us) and when I finished—I was finished with my month's assignment in the first
week—and I wasn't even asked to turn in a written report.

But don't let me discourage you. For when a consultant
is called in by a well managed, profitable company with a
specific manufacturing, designing, or marketing problem, his
expertise in that specific area can be most satisfying to the
consultant and productive to the client.

Consultants soon find that over-retirement-age is absolutely a plus, rather than a minus. In fact, the older you get
to be, the larger the fee you get to get. There are many reasons for the popularity of retirees as consultants. More important, the executives in the company are not worried that
you might be replacing one of them. Therefore, they will co-
operate fully with an over-age consultant. No departmental
executive can be as comfortable with a 40 year old consul-

tant who is an expert in the executive's field, and is reporting on that executive's department directly to the President.

So I maintain, the consulting field is the most prestigious, lucrative, and opportunistic field for the ex-executive retiree.

* * * * * * * * * * * * * *

A few years ago I heard a speaker claim that the average life span for an executive after retirement is only three years and nine months. I do not give much credence even to our government's documented statistics, because they are incomplete in the first place and are based on yesterday's figures. So I don't believe the speaker because his figure is so far below the average 17 year expectancy for the 65 year old male. No doubt his purpose was to shock the audience, and he succeeded since I still remember the figure although I have forgotten the speaker.

The three year nine month figure may apply to top decision making executives in a particularly stressful industry, but perhaps I find it difficult to accept because it would mean that I am way past my lay down time. But then I find comfort in the knowledge that, having followed the tenets of this book, I retired early and am very busy doing what I have always wanted to do.

If the three year nine month figure is fallacious, why do I keep dwelling on it? Because I am a believer that many executives do expire sooner after retirement than the non-executive retiree, for an executive without a plan for working after retirement, is like a valuable race horse put out to stud without any mares. So the point made by that speaker is correct, and if my elaboration will shock even one executive into changing careers and thereby prolong his retired life, I will have achieved my purpose.

Too late for K.D.
PROFILE OF K.D.

Retired at age 50 with five million dollars.

K.D. was a successful manufacturer who got the message
when one of his closest buddies died at age 48. The message was, "You can't take it with you, so why kill yourself
making more money than you can spend?" So he sold out
for five million and planned to enjoy the hereafter.

He was a member of the city's most prestigious country
clubs, which prior to retiring was his occasional golf play-
ground. Now it became his daily hangout for everyday golf,
a few drinks, lunch, a few drinks, etc. But his friends all had
to get back to their work, so K.D. had to drink alone—
which he did.

After one year, his wife sued for divorce. They were certainly not compatible as they did nothing together.

Now with no wife to come home to—he didn't. And by the
end of the second year, K.D. was a hopeless despicable
drunk. From boistrous antagonistic alcoholic fits, he gradu-
ated to drunken stupors, falling into stagnating sleep at the
bar, in the locker room and in his car. Now he no longer
was welcome in his country club.

He died at age 53.

RATING BY J.S.: With a prospect of 35% of his life span
ahead of him, this man had made no plans for living.

Some of my friends who have read this profile before publication, were sure they knew whom I was referring to. (I
always use fictitious initials.) But the men they knew were
not my K.D. So I must conclude that this is not as unusual
a case as I thought.

* * * * * * * * * * * * *

The carpenter, the plumber, and the auto mechanic will never be a three year nine month statistic, for they are needed by the neighbor whose plumbing or whose car breaks down. At first, the retired plumber will assist the neighbor and refuse compensation. One day the neighbor will say, "Jim, I want to be able to call on you whenever I need you. I want to pay you so that I will feel I'm not sponging, and since you won't charge me regular plumber's rates, we are both better off." So the ex-plumber finds he is needed and his retirement is fulfilling and compensating.

But if the plumber dislikes plumbing and has always wanted to do cabinet work, he gets his workshop set up and is soon involved in making furniture for himself, and for his neighbors, and for money.

But executives are also in demand by their neighbors. The Service Corps of Retired Executives (SCORE) assists small business enterprises who have problems or who are threatened with imminent failure. SCORE recruits and assigns the retired executive to the company that has a need for his administrative guidance in its particular field. It might be the corner liquor store or a manufacturing plant, or an SBA financed minority business—somewhere out in retirementland is the answer. Although this does not provide compensation other than expenses, many ex-executives enjoy the challenge and especially the opportunity of proving their executive ability.

Or how about getting into an essential and inflation proof business? Income property—apartment buildings, to be specific. I am prejudiced since I am so involved, but I firmly believe that this is an ideal business for any person to retire to. And if such statistics were available, I am certain it would prove that a large percentage of apartment buildings in this country are now owned by people like you and me.

It is a dignified business filling an important social need. Owning/operating/and even living in your own building gives a retired person purpose, economic stability, and roots.

CHAPTER X

AFTER RETIREMENT

go to work so you can retire again

Looking for a new career is exciting. How long has it been since you were free to answer an ad or knock on a prospective employer's door?

For those of you who know exactly what you want to do, since you've known it for years, you must be chomping at the bit. If you have always wanted to paint, write, or be a sculptor, it's easy: Get some brushes, or paper, or a chisel, and get started.

For those of you who want to go into business for yourself, it's easy if you have the necessary investment capital, otherwise, it's a little harder to do—and maybe, just maybe not the smart thing to do on borrowed capital. Age does make a difference when you are thinking of mortgaging all you have for a try at a business venture. At age 45, G.W. did, and he is glad he did.

PROFILE OF G.W.

He retired at age 60—and so did she.

G.W. worked for many years in the artist supply department of a large stationery store. He was fortunate to find his work to be fun, and he enjoyed sharing his customer's dreams, hopes, and despairs.

When he was 45 his employer sold out. The new owner planned to convert the store to office furniture and supplies and no longer handle art materials. G.W. was asked to remain for a few months to aid in liquidating the inventory of his department.

Mrs. G.W. suggested that G.W. go off salary and operate the art department as a concessionaire—paying rent and a percentage of sales. The proposition was accepted on a trial basis and G.W. arranged a bank loan to purchase the inventory.

With little capital, a large bank loan, and no funds for employee payroll, Mrs. G.W. had to work in the store on a temporary basis. The venture was successful and the working team of Mr. and Mrs. was sensational. Their home life had always been exemplary, and now that togetherness was actually on a 24 hour schedule, they were even happier than before. So the temporary deal became a permanent full time operation that lasted for 15 years.

G.W. told me they did no pre-retirement planning. They decided to sell out when he reached 60 and never worried about their future life style. Retirement meant no change for they enjoy being together 24 hours a day.

RATING BY J.S.: G.W. found a full time cause—The City of Hope. They had always supported this outstanding medical research and hospital facility and now they became totally involved.

I am fortunate that not all wedded couples are 24 hour compatible. For if they were, there would be no need for books purporting to solve non-existent problems.

* * * * * * * * * * * * * *

For you who must begin to supplement your income soon, take heart, for you are lucky too. ANYONE WHO WANTS TO WORK—CAN. JOBS ARE NOT ALWAYS AVAILABLE, BUT WORK ALWAYS IS.

When you were a kid, did you like to play cops and robbers? When you were grown up and you got a ticket for speeding, didn't you wish you were a cop; So, here's your chance, be a

Bank Guard. 90% of the bank guards are retired or moonlighters soon to retire. Pay isn't great, but you can kiss your wife goodbye for a few hours a day. Much easier (and safer) work than lugging the shopping bags from the Supermarket. And you get to wear a uniform, and the pretty tellers call you "Pop." And it's a lot less dangerous than flying to Miami and ending up in Uganda. (If you're a woman and you want the job, just whisper discrimination and you'll get it.)

Or were you in the Shmata business (also known as the rag business or the ladies ready-to-wear)? Maybe you were Vice-President in Charge of, or you had your own little store until Sears and even Safeway Supermarkets started to carry ladies blouses and slacks amidst the salami and bologna. Get even with them by joining up with a giant

Department Store. Again minimum wages for clerking, but how long can one watch television? Besides it gives you a chance to eat lunch with someone else's spouse who is glad to get away from her spouse.

Or perhaps you are tired of regular hours and want a
complete change, but you are not a loner since you do enjoy the company of other people. This makes you a likely
candidate for a meaningful, tax sheltered reducing your
living-costs job as an

Apartment Building Manager. A small building
will provide you a discount on your own apartment. A medium size building will give you a free
apartment. A large project will give you a free
apartment, utilities, telephone, plus a monthly
salary of $100 to $250.

None of the above will usually interfere with your
Social Security income. And your functions can be
limited to collecting rents, showing and re-renting,
with no maintenance or cleaning chores. However
if you (or your spouse) are handy with tools, you
might arrange to do the light maintenance work for
additional compensation.

If you are not yet eligible for Social Security and/
or you don't mind being tied down to regular office hours, you can find larger apartment complexes that will pay sizable salaries in addition to
the free apartment and fringe benefits.

Are these opportunities available?

Just look in your local newspaper's classified section under "Couples Wanted."

This is also an excellent area for a single mature
person of either sex. It is a people business which
keeps one from being bored and cures the disease
of loneliness.

Or if you were in sales, you must realize that oppor-
tunites are especially available to you, for this is the field
where older age is a plus instead of a minus. Buyers tend to
be more relaxed and have more confidence in dealing with a
mature salesperson. And whether our economy is in a de-

pressive state or booming, inflation or deflation, rain or shine
—there are always openings for
Commission Sales Personnel. And don't forget the
tax benefits. You are legitimately entitled to business deductions for auto expense, telephone, etc.,
and you can continue to build Social Security cre-
dits. Thousands of public employees who retire at
45 or 50 with a substantial pension, have gone into
sales which earns for them, in many instances, an
additional pension income. So take your choice
Real Estate
Insurance
Automobiles, or how about the
Direct Selling Field? This is the oldest form of free
enterprise and the start of many of our largest and
oldest companies. It is a vast area where anyone
can be an independent businessman with little or
no investment. Over three million direct sales representatives of all ages, from college students,
housewives, to retired, earn the income they desire (whether pin-money or substantial) plus enjoy-
ing the convenience of establishing their own work
ing hours. And the public, as a whole, must appreciate the convenience of buying reputable products
in the privacy and comfort of their home, for they
appreciate it to the extent of six billion dollars
each year.
Some of the larger well-known companies are
Amway Corporation
Avon Products
Encyclopaedia Britannica, Inc.
Family Record Plan, Inc.
Fuller Brush Company
Grolier Incorporated
Mason Shoe Manufacturing Co.
Shaklee Corporation
Wear-Ever Aluminum, Inc.
If you can't find the product you wish to sell, send

inquiry to
> Direct Selling Association
> 1730 M Street, N.W.
> Washington, D.C. 20036

Direct Selling is one industry that provides an equal opportunity for everyone regardless of race, creed, color, age, sex, and even physical impairment.

Everyone of these companies has successful representatives who are older than you, and who are more physically impaired than you. All you need is the will and they will provide the way. Yes, I am a great booster for Direct Sales, for that was my pre-retirement life's work. And I was proud of my role as a salesman, for sales are what make the wheels go round, in an industrialized society. Nothing happens in business until and unless a sale is made. The man in the factory, the executive, the secretary—not one of them would have a job if it were not for the person who sells their product.

And no salesperson on commission is ever faced with mandatory retirement because of age. (My apologies to Arthur Miller, author of "Death Of A Salesman"—Willy just needed a change of territory.) Or Willy should have met D.A.—I'm glad I did.

PROFILE OF D.A.

Retired at 60, eighteen years ago. Retired again at age 70—might retire again at ?.

This remarkable lady proves that women not only outlive men but they can outwork them also.

D.A. retired at 60 from school teaching to take an executive position with a small company that she helped form two years previously. She worked there for ten years until the company was merged into one of the giant international conglomerates—and of course, she was shelved and pensioned off as the grand old lady. So she took a job as a commission salesperson (where age doesn't matter) and each of the last eight years she has qualified for the company conventions. (Incidentally, it is the same company that put her out to pasture, for she was too old.)

Widowed 25 years ago, but she is not lonely since she can always ring another door bell and visit—and sell. D.A. claims that she works nights because it is more fun (and profitable) than watching TV.

RATING BY J.S.: Are you kidding? How would you rate a gal of 78 who collects her teacher's pension; company pension; Social Security; plus a sizable commission? *A PLUS!*

CHAPTER XI

STAY ON DAYLIGHT SAVINGS TIME
and loosen your shoelaces

There are certain beliefs attributed to the process of aging that are true, yet they are also false. For example, older people will tell you that the days, weeks, months, years seem to be shorter, and that time goes by more quickly as one gets older.

Retirees immediately notice this strange phenomenon, for it is true—the days are shorter. I noticed it when I retired, and practically every retiree that I have questioned agrees that the days are definitely shorter.

Of course they are! Before retirement, we got up at the break of day, 6 or 7 A.M., dressed, showered, breakfasted, rode or walked to work, and we worked during the hours of nine to five. Eight hours at work plus three hours getting up and to and fro = 11 hours, so the day was 11 hours long.

The first day after I retired, there was no need to get up early, so I partook of the luxury of staying in bed, and I got up at 8 A.M.—so my first day was shortened by two hours. The next day, I slept until 8:30. The third day I was tired, so I slept until 9; and then 9:30; then 10 A.M.—now my day was only seven daylight hours long.

My days were definitely shorter and the weeks were passing more quickly. But it wasn't long before I realized that it wasn't *time* going faster, but *me* going slower. So I began to arise before 8 A.M. and by increasing my daylight hours, I slowed old father time down (and so can you).

* * * * * * * * * * * * *

Another strange belief is that a man doesn't look his age prior to retiring, but on that very day, when the world knows he is 65, he looks his age. Actually, it happens one day after his 65th birthday, for he is freshly bathed, shaven and dressed in his finest, for his birthday cake.

The next day he doesn't shave. He doesn't put on a suit and tie. For the first time, that any neighbor can recollect, he goes out to pick up the newspaper off the lawn at 9 A.M. (instead of 7 A.M.) *and in his undershirt.*

Is this bad? No, I think it is good to stop dressing and behaving as though you were in competition with youth. We've all done that at some time in our business life, and retirement means you don't need to, any longer. Act your age, and look your age. Maturity is beautiful and respectable. But don't get sloppy. Don't stop shaving and don't stop bathing. You are not alone, even if without kith or kin. There are people all around you. Your age has earned for you the right to relax, loaf, golf, or work. Don't wear suits and ties, if you don't want to. Put on your loafers and sport shirts. Get comfortable. But don't get, "Oh, to hell with it" sloppy.

And this applies also to the thousands of women, who go through the hells of self-torture during the 15 years prior to retirement. We all know the sixtyish steno who spends hours each day on her hair, make up, one calorie drinks, cottage cheese, up at 6 A.M. in order to be the first at her desk at 10 minutes before 9—hating each passing day, dreading the threatened boredom of home all day. What a price she pays, as she struggles to keep up with the kids, when she should, instead, proudly look, act, and dress her age. For she should look forward to retirement as an exciting change, and plan for it, so that she can truly welcome an even earlier retirement date.

* * * * * * * * * * * * * *

As one gets older, one supposes one must have constant doctoring. One who does not believe one must, is I. And many doctors agree with me, since they estimate that one out of every three calls for medical treatment have no organic basis, but are psychosomatic.

In this age of ultra-specialized sophisticated medicine, it is interesting that there is a growing tendency to go back to simplistic medicine. The belated recognition of the remedial power of chicken soup (Jewish penicillin) is an extreme example of the latest trend. Holistic medicine and non-traditional approaches to medical care, such as biofeedback, acupuncture, and guided imagery are gaining the attention of medical educators and scientists. This makes me believe that the world is ready for the most unsophisticated, untraditional self-care health movement of all—CAUSISTIC MEDICINE. I am solely responsible for the name *causistic,* but the practice of causistic medicine is as old as Man, who discovered that the thorn in the sole of his foot caused pain—and that by removing the cause, he was rid of the pain.

When you were working, you did not go to the doctor often. You didn't even have time for your annual check-up. Besides, all he ever told you was what you already knew. You were fine, except a few pounds overweight.

Now that you are retired, you have plenty of time, and you know something is bound to be wrong. And what the heck, you've got Medicare. So you become a hyper-self-concentrator (a retired hypochondriac). You had a strange ache last night, or you got dizzy watching TV. Many of your aches and pains are real at that moment, but curable by you. Think back to *just before* the ache—THE CAUSE. The cure is as simple as getting a larger size collar, and no more pain in the neck; or getting trousers with a waist measure of 38 instead of 36, and no more pain in the belly. I'm not kidding!

After I retired I developed an excrutiating pain in my right shoulder. Suspecting bursitis, the doctor advised that if it persisted, I should get cortisone shots. But I have always researched my ailments in my Schiffere's Family Medical Encyclopedia. It said, "bursitis ... a typical example is 'housemaid's knee.' " If I were the housemaid, I imagined I could alleviate my hurt, by stand-up mopping instead of kneeling. So since my right shoulder was hurting, I tried sleeping on my left side. (Did I remember to tell you, that I always slept on my right side? I can't sleep on my left side.) But to my surprise, I slept the whole night on my left side. I know, because every time I shifted to my right, I would hurt, so back to my left. After two weeks of sleeping on my left, I no longer had any bursitis in my right shoulder.

My second case of causistic medicine. Last year, my luck ran out. My toes on my left foot were killing me. Every night I soaked my foot in epsom salts, and exercised my toes. In the morning I felt better, but by nightfall, I had the same constant pain. I knew this had to be the result of my over-indulgence—I had gout. But my bursitis incident was fresh in my memory, so I searched for a reason, other than, "It's time I had something wrong with me," and I realized that I had been wearing a new pair of shoes. I changed to my old shoes, and in 48 hours, the gout was gone. The new shoes were too short.

My third confession will explain why I was so smart as to have causistically treated my bursitis and gout. One morning (about 25 years ago) I passed blood when answering nature's call. This was so unusual, and with the fear of cancer in mind, I immediately sought out a specialist in proctology. He diagnosed it as hemorrhoids and recommended immediate surgery. To delay could be serious. He finally agreed to a one week reprieve so I could get my business affairs in order. But the next day there was no bleeding. And the following day, again no blood. And I checked my medical home dictionary and discovered that hemorrhoids were as common as tonsils. And so, I am still intact at both ends.

So, I'm not kidding, when I alert retirees to LOOK FOR THE CAUSE. Don't abuse Medicare, and yourself, by being treated for hurts that might be attributed to a new, and too hard mattress.

If you are leg-weary and your feet hurt, loosen your shoelaces. If your shoes have no laces but are the comfortable slip-ons or buckle-ups, and your feet hurt—change to shoes with laces, and loosen the laces. If I am right, then you were restricting your circulation. If I am wrong, then you have another pair of uncomfortable shoes *with laces*.

An older person does not have to acquire arthritis, bursitis, gout or senility. If you helped your neighbor move his refrigerator, you used some muscles that you had not called upon since you played football in college, so you are bound to have a new ache. And, if you have truly retired, as per Webster's definition, you've got plenty of time to enjoy your new ache.

7 Part I—Tues., Aug. 22, 1978   Los Angeles Times

THICK WALLETS A PAIN

Doctor Picks Pockets to Cure Backache

CHICAGO (AP)—If you come to Dr. Elmar G. Lutz complaining of back pains, he will ask to see your wallet before he gives you an X ray—but not because he wonders whether you can afford the bill.

Lutz, of St. Mary's Hospital in Passaic, N.J., reported the results of an unusual treatment in a letter in the Aug. 25 edition of the Journal of the American Medical Assn.

In the first of the two cases described, a 56-year-old patient complained of having had back pains for 14 months. Lutz noticed that he carried a thick wallet in the back pocket. It was 1½ inches thick, filled with credit cards the man used in his travels as a salesman.

"Walletectomy resulted in fairly immediate and complete relief," Lutz said.

The other patient, a 35-year-old man, had a sedentary occupation and said he had had pains for eight years in his right thigh and lower back. He suffered from numbness in the right foot also.

Transfer of his inch-thick wallet, also filled with credit cards, from his hip pocket to his jacket pocket relieved him of his pains.

Lutz said that he had encountered similar cases in previous years, leading him to suspect that such back pains might be caused by thick wallets. He suggested that physicians be alert to this to eliminate unnecessary X ray and other diagnostic studies.

Reprinted by permission of Associated Press

CHAPTER XII

A COUPLE WILL BE A SINGLE SOMEDAY

because it's only temporary, never permanent

Many a mature senior couple are immature, because they will not discuss the inevitability that one will die before the other. When I asked a number of acquaintances whether they had ever discussed this matter, I have had this type of reply from a number of them. "We hope that we both die at the same time. We've had a good marriage and I don't want to live after John (or Ida) dies. So I pray that I go at the same time."

This attitude is their way of professing love for one's spouse and telling the world they have had an ideal relationship. *But it is the biggest lie of all time.* For the truth is that the survivor will live and will fight to live even though his loved companion is gone. The instinct for survival stays with

us all of our life and that is normal, moral, and laudible. I
believe the following personal experience is a perfect example of the instinct to survive.

My wife is disabled due to a stroke and completely
dependent upon me and/or her live-in companion.
She has always said and to this very day says, "I
hope and pray that I die before my husband does,
or at least at the same time, for I cannot face life
without him."
So when I learned that I must undergo emergency
surgery, I was most apprehensive as to how to
break the news to my wife. Since her stroke, she
has been uncontrollably emotional whenever any
problem of that nature affected anyone of the
family. I had never had surgery of any kind, nor
had I ever spent an hour in any hospital as a patient, so I knew this would be a terrible, traumatic
shock to my wife. I waited until an hour before I
had to leave for the hospital. I alerted our com-
panion/homemaker. I warned her to expect my
wife to break down and I had the smelling salts
ready in case she fainted. Hesitantly I began,
"Honey, I have to go into the hospital for minor
surgery."
"What do you mean? What kind of surgery?"
"Oh, just the usual male problem, prostate."
"Is there a chance of malignancy?"
"Always a possibility, but the doctor says he's
quite sure I'll be okay."
"When are you going in?"
"Right now, in fact I'm leaving in 30 minutes.
Might as well get it over with, but you'll be okay
because Stella will be with you every minute until
I get home."
And instead of my wife breaking down hysterical-
ly, she surprised me by saying in a calm voice
"How much money is there in the house? Which

checkbook can I draw checks on?"
And when I waved goodbye, she waved back just
as self-possessed as if I were going to the supermarket.

* * * * * * * * * * * * * *

I do not believe my father and mother ever discussed
or planned for the day one might die. If they did, they never
told any one of their children of their plans.

However, my wife's mother and father did discuss it
and they told their three children of their decision many
times. They decided that the survivor would come to live
with me and their daughter, and when it happened—he did.

I suggest that pre-death planning is an important part of
pre-retirement and post-retirement planning. For although
my mother-in-law's death was sudden and unexpected, her
grief stricken 71 year old spouse immediately moved into our
home without the family conferences and arguments as to
who takes the old man in and for how long. It also spared
him the uncertainty of whether or not to break up his home
for he knew his wife would have approved his move. But
never plan for the rest of the survivor's life, for the survivor will get over his grief and he might wish to live, too.

If you have children, who in turn have their own, and
if you are so inclined *and so close,* tell them your choice, and
if you know your children and in-laws as well as you should,
your decision will be respected. I warn you though, if your
estate is a substantial fortune, tell your choice in advance
only to the chosen one. Don't tell the others until it happens.
Otherwise you may have years of estranged family relations,
as the other children and their spouses will think this means
that the chosen one is going to inherit all of your estate. But
never plan nor commit yourselves to living with a child permanently. Permanent can be a long time and even the most

considerate parent can wear out his welcome. And no single, no matter what age, should resign himself/or herself to remaining single permanently.

Better yet, if you, the older folks, have a home that is more spacious and nicer than the home of the chosen one, consider offering that they (when the expected unexpectantly occurs) come *live in your home.* Don't sign your home over to your children *now* or *then.* But if they are making your house a home for you and them, for as long as you live, you should bequeath it to them.

Have you ever noticed that an older lady without money is said to be mentally unstable when she does something unusually odd. The same lady with money would be called eccentric.

And an older man who forgets something is called senile, unless he is wealthy, for then he is said to have something else on his mind.

Never, never transfer your home and assets to your children as long as one of you two is still alive. An old man or an old woman is an elderly gentleman or an elderly lady as long as he or she is able to buy birthday and Christmas presents for the children and grandchildren. I believe in assisting children financially while you are both alive and can enjoy seeing the results of your help *but never give until it hurts.*

I know of one couple who are not wealthy but they are living comfortably on their Social Security and, most important, the interest earnings on their sizable savings and loan accounts. They are able to meet their financial needs without ever touching their capital. They advised their children never to purchase an automobile or furniture, etc., on the time plan, and pay the high interest rates charged for installment purchases. Grandma and grandpa would lend them the funds so that they could pay cash. However it was with the definite understanding that the child would sign a note at the same interest rate as the savings and loan is paying on the account—and the child would pay monthly installments to the same savings and loan account. Result—the children save a substantial amount of interest, and the savings account is replenished. Perhaps because the borrower gets a monthly notice from the savings and loan, the borrowers, I am told, have never missed one payment on its due date. They added, that a number of times the loans have been renegotiated upward, but never has a monthly payment been delinquent.

The parents tell me that the children appreciate this arrangement because it is business-like. They do not feel that they are imposing nor do they have to beg for assistance, and yet they know that the folks are helping them financially. And every penny paid back into the savings account will one day be returned to the children when the estate is finally apportioned.

On the other hand, if you are wealthy, then not one of your children should be forced to live poorly merely because you feel they should prove to you that they can make it on their own. For they will get it all when you die, and if you make them wait for assistance until you die—they will hate you for living so long.

CHAPTER XIII

A WIDOWER HAS A CHOICE

for he can be a couple any day

Don't live alone. There is no reason for any man to live alone if he can walk, talk, tie his own shoelaces, and pay his own way.

The only one more lonely than a lonely older woman is a lonely older man.

As I said earlier, if you have a son or daughter with whom you can live comfortably without disrupting his or her life, fine. But it is difficult for an older person to move into a child's home without disruption, no matter how ideal the situation may appear to be. So I will repeat: If you do it, do it only on a temporary and not a permanent basis. Tell them at the outset that you appreciate being welcome to share their home, but that you will eventually want to get back to your own quarters. For no matter how close you may be with your daughter or son, your living with one of them does call for compromises by all parties (especially in-laws).

However, if your house is more spacious and desirable than your child's residence, and he and his spouse accept your invitation to live with you, there is an excellent chance of permanency.

* * * * * * * * * * * * * *

So when my mother-in-law passed away, my 71 year old father-in-law moved in with his daughter and son-in-law. We had a large five bedroom, four bathroom empty nest, so space was no problem. And my wife was the most considerate daughter, a most considerate father was ever blessed to have. Pop enjoyed his meals. He never left the house in the morning without ordering his choice for dinner. And after a while, this began to irritate me just a little bit. When my wife served steak to her father and meat loaf to me, I protested in private but was told, "Pop is an old man. He ordered steak and you've always said you preferred meat loaf to steak. After all, what's he got to live for, but his meals. You're a young man—you have everything to live for."
I countered with "I don't want you to cook different dishes for your father. This is not a restaurant so I'll eat what he likes and he can eat what I like."
But one night my wife cooked a tongue and placed it on the table in its original shape and form (I never could take tongue even when sliced and hidden between two slices of bread)—from then on, I no longer insisted on one dish for all.
Every morning at 7:30 A.M. his son picked Pop up to take him to work at his son's business. And

every Friday night Pop would pay my wife $20, for he was not a free-loader. Pop had plenty of girl friends who would invite him over for seven course meals, but he always resisted their let's make it permanent proposals because he said he had a lovely home and a marvelous housekeeper, and he would always add that he was too old to remarry, for how long did he have to live? And every birthday he reminded us of that. "And why should I get married to an old sick woman that I might have to take care of?"

But never was a man more wrong. He could have, and he should have remarried at age 72 and both his and my life would have been very different.

When Pop was 78, he married his wife's sister, a 77 year old sickly widow who looked like his former wife's twin. She had come to our home to spend the winter in California and to keep house for Pop while my wife and I took an extended European trip. When we got back, Pop announced they were going to get married and set up their own apartment. So my wife began to drive her Dad and his 77 year old fiancee shopping for new furniture, linens, kitchenware, etc.—and they were fussy kids—everything had to be just the way they wanted because they never before had everything new and they would not settle for second best.

After three weeks of dutiful daughter's driving, shopping, and redecorating Pop's new apartment, my wife was on the verge of collapse. Pop and Aunt Rose were married on Saturday night and planned to move to their own apartment the following Saturday, but they never made it. For Aunt Rose collapsed and died on the floor of our home on Tuesday.

That same evening, Pop asked my wife, "What's for dinner?" My wife, still in shock with grief said, "Dad, how can you think of dinner when Aunt

Rose has been gone only a few hours?" Pop answered, "Daughter, when people get to my age, death is to be expected at any moment. I made her happy for a short time for she knew she was wanted. But the living must live, and to live, one must eat"—and he did.

But my wife did not get over the shock. After going through another harrowing two weeks of returning new unused furniture, linens, wedding gifts, etc., my wife suffered a massive heart attack.

Now with a wife with a heart problem and a father-in-law who could no longer maneuver the stairs with safety, I decided to sell my three story home and move to a one floor apartment. We moved twice during the next three years to apartments that were not my choice, but they were near bus stops so that Pop could get to his house of worship.

We got along very well. My wife recovered completely from her heart attack, but Pop's legs were beginning to fail. He no longer took the bus for he had difficulty walking. During the 11 years that Pop lived with us, he repeatedly proclaimed that there was a time for everything, and that the day he could no longer tie his shoelaces or take a bath unaided, he himself would select a rest home, for he would never impose or be a burden to anyone—and I believed him.

The day finally arrived when my wife suggested that I, from then on, should assist Pop in and out of the bathtub. I protested, saying that Pop always said that when that day came, he would seek out a rest home. But my wife replied, "I'm sure he doesn't mean it, and after all, he's an old man. How long has he got?"

I answered, "I am not a male nurse. He has lived with us for 11 years and I have never complained, but this is the end of the line. I have shared my wife long enough. You have a choice to make. You can live with me or your father, but no longer with both."

I was 56 years old at the time, and my wife was 54. In our 35 years of marriage, we obviously had some disagreements but we had never had a serious argument. This was the closest we ever came to an argument. We talked on and on until 1 A.M. but I was adamant. The next day, my wife suffered a stroke.

Now my father-in-law had no choice but to move, and two weeks after Pop moved to a plush retirement home—he was dead.

I could get mawkish at this point, but I won't. What then is the point of my telling it all? Some may say it's my guilt complex showing. Maybe it is. I do believe that my dispute with my wife about her father brought on the stroke. The doctors say "No," but I'll never believe them.

Maybe I'm trying to put the blame on Pop, believing that if he had not lived with us, we wouldn't have argued or have had the emotional upheaval, and the stroke never would have occurred. Maybe. Who can say?

I guess the point is, that I now know that Pop—as wonderful, considerate, and loving a father as ever walked the earth—Pop was wrong. At age 75, when Pop shook your hand, you had to check your fingers to make certain they were not broken. He was a vital, vigorous man who in his 70's had the stamina of a man of 50. He worked every day until 81. He was financially and physically able to have had his own life and his own new wife. But because of his love for his children and closeness with his family, and perhaps a fear of new beginnings in his older years, he was blind to the devastating effects of overstaying his welcome and becoming a burden.

* * * * * * * * * * * * * * *

I must proclaim now LOUD and CLEAR—for of this, I am certain—NO FAMILY NEED EVER FEEL ONE TWINGE OF GUILT if their mother or father is confined to a total-care institution, if that person can no longer take care of his own personal needs.

AND NO PARENT SHOULD EXPECT ANY YOUNGER GENERATION FAMILY MEMBER to give up his active life for a caretaking existence.

And so, my wife and I have discussed what we should do after one of us dies. And we have agreed, that we are never going to live with our son and daughter-in-law. But we also have agreed, and have so notified our son and his wife, that if they should *at that time*, wish to live in our apartment (or in another apartment in our building), they would be most welcome to do so. For since we own the building, and it will be their's someday—they might as well—and I'll bet they will—someday.

CHAPTER XIV

A WOMAN HAS A CHOICE
unless she prefers not to

There are many women of all ages, who are unhappy with their single life, and maybe this chapter will put a little adventure in some of the older women's souls, and some purpose in the adventure.

I admit this will be of no interest to the women who truly prefer to live alone, and to those ensnared in miserable marriages who wish they had never moved out of their bachelor apartments. If you are in this category, it's O.K. with me if you skip this chapter and go on to the next.

* * * * * * * * * * * * * *

I direct this mainly to the millions of unemployed widows and divorcees. There are millions of men and women (singles and couples) who desperately need you, and are anxious to provide employment—and, in many cases, companionship (someone to talk to is companionship). I'm not touting the "playboy" or "playgirl" type of companionship—although I am not knocking it either. But I warn you, as with any job, apartment, clothes, or car, etc., don't buy without checking carefully, for some will be to your liking, and some won't.

The group of women I refer to are the "displaced homemakers." According to the Alliance of Displaced Homemakers, over 2.2 million women were in that category, way back in March 1973. Due to the increase in the divorce rate and the longer life expectancy of women, the 2.2 million figure is now estimated to be 3 to 7 million.

According to the Alliance, the definition of a displaced homemaker is an individual
(a) who has been doing unpaid labor in the home;
(b) who is not gainfully employed;
(c) who has had, or would have difficulty in securing employment;
(d) and who has been dependent on the income of another family member but is no longer supported by that income.

The Committee on Education and Labor, House of Representatives, held hearings in regard to suggested legislation dealing with this problem. One of the major considerations was the establishment of training centers throughout the country to train displaced homemakers to be skilled job-seekers as typists, bookkeepers, etc., in business and industry. But I maintain, most of these wives and mothers are already skilled as homemakers. No one will disagree that there are many jobs available for homemakers in motherless and disabled person's homes. It is a noble profession, and although never considered a job when performed by a family member, it is certainly recognized and appreciated as a most essential service when furnished by and for a non-family person.

I do not disagree with the problem and the need for a solution. I disagree with our government's solution. I disagree with the notion that *all* skilled homemakers (a field that has many job openings and where older age is an asset) should be trained to be office workers (a field that has fewer jobs and where youth is paramount).

I am not against the up-grading of a skilled homemaker to any other skilled position one might aspire to. I am against the *down-grading* of the skill of the homemaking profession by our governmental agencies.

* * * * * * * * * * * * *

Here is a typical ad in the classified section of your daily newspaper.

FREE—To one mature unencumbered lady. Live in a furnished home, good meals if you are a good cook, TV, conversation, leisure time. The catch is that a gentleman (65) lives and eats here too and pays all expenses plus fair salary for homemaking duties. References exchanged. Telephone 888-8888.

I call upon all displaced homemakers (without minor children) to compare the above job opportunity against your present situation. You are not employed, therefore no regular paycheck. You live in a single or one bedroom apartment, rent $200 monthly, food $100. You no longer have anyone to cook for; no one to talk to; and you fear living alone. If the advertised job pays $250 a month, you are really earning $550 per month (because you no longer pay the $200 for rent or the $100 for food). Since you have very few expenses, you should be able to bank at least $300 each month, which in ten years with interest should accumulate to over

$47,000. And if you are drawing old age Social Security benefits, you can continue to do so, since you are within the allowable earnings limitation. Whereas if you got an office job paying you $550, you could not continue to receive your full Social Security benefits (and after paying for rent and food, you are not nearly so well off).

Obviously, all of the above must be based on certain assumptions. The gentleman must be someone you can not only endure, but one whose company you enjoy, and whose countenance you don't mind seeing across the dinner table. And he must be a person who does not cause you to put a deadbolt on your bedroom door. But this too brings up an important point. How companionable can companionship become? Society recognizes the human need for food, drink, sleep, and love. And if such an arrangement should develop into the ultimate intimate relationship, whose business is it? Whom are you hurting? And if it leads to the formality of marriage and caring and love, fine! A displaced homemaker is no longer displaced, and a lonely widower is no longer lonely. Isn't this what most mature singles genuinely hope for and seldom achieve, because they do not have the opportunity of a close inter-dependent one-to-one relationship?

And let's not forget there are many displaced home-makers age 35 with a young dependent child. Suppose the same type of ad appeared saying it was "a motherless home with two angelic children." What better way of solving two families problems? I say—answer that ad right away before someone else beats you to it.

If being a homemaker for a single man seems too bold, too unconventional, too "what will my family think?"—then answer the ad of a Senior Citizen couple. This will still be rated by our heavenly Father as a mitzvah (a mitzvah is a good deed deserving of a blessing).

If words like alms, charity, and dole could be changed

to welfare, and welfare be considered a right; so can the words domestic, servant, maid, and housekeeper be changed to homemaker, and homemaker be considered a noble profession. For there is no more useful or worthwhile work that one could perform than to make a house of a lonely single person or a house of an impaired elderly couple into an efficient companionable home.

It makes economic good sense, social good sense and, most important of all, human good sense. It makes no sense at all, that our government does not have sense enough to recognize the job opportunities in this area.

* * * * * * * * * * * * * * *

Retirement homes are filled with thousands of able-bodied men and women who because of convention are committed to life sentences of resignation and unhappiness. If every such retirement hostel would pair up every able bodied man and woman in one bedroom units (with refrigerator and stove), many a couple would realize that they have enough steam to get out and set up housekeeping once again.

Do you think I am just trying to shock you? Think again. A state social service official recently recommended that older folks in rest homes and public institutions should be allowed more privacy for sexual activity. Why not housekeeping activity as well?

The coupling of compatible consenting Seniors in their own apartments instead of the routing of singles to institutions would save millions of dollars. Any single is a candidate for a more prolonged hospital stay merely because he or she lives alone. They remain in the hospital at over $100 a day because there is no one at home to prepare the meals while recuperating. And the $100+ a day, whether paid by Medicare, Blue Cross, or welfare is a waste of millions that would be saved if Mary had a Benjamin to come home to.

My mother died at age 79. My father took it very
hard. After two years, we finally got him to venture out to Florida to escape the cold New Hampshire winter.

He dreaded going alone, and would not have, but
another home town widower knew the ropes
since he was a three winter veteran and he took
Dad in tow. The second year, we did not have to
urge Dad to go, for now he knew the ropes. (I did
not know what knowing the ropes meant—I
found out it meant that any loose unattached man
age 65 to 102 was forever being invited to a free
home cooked dinner by an over 70 year old unattached gal.)

The third winter, my 84 year old Dad became
senile and should have been committed to an institution, according to the emergency phone calls
I received from my sisters.

"Dad wants to get married. He met some young
broad who is going to take him for all he's got.
He's gone crazy. You must fly to Miami and stop
him."

My Dad had about $10,000 savings, his Social
Security checks, a pot belly, a hacking cigarette
cough, a prostate problem, and a beautiful hippie
head of hair.

So I phoned Dad and he didn't sound nuts at all.
He sounded younger and happier than usual. I
asked him (after the usual pleasantries) how old
the prospective bride was, and he said, "I don't
know—about 75, I guess."

So I gave him my blessings, and my sisters
wouldn't speak to me for a year.

It is now seven years later. My father is 91 years
old. His wife is a delight.

They care for each other deeply, although I assure
you, my Dad is the luckier of the two. Two
months ago, I got the inevitable phone call—Dad

was in the hospital, pneumonia, oxygen tank—it was the end. My brother flew over to make the final arrangements and accompany the body home to New Hampshire, and I was about to get my airline ticket to attend the services.

My brother had to stay eight days, for Dad wasn't ready to go on his last flight. Finally, since they could not tolerate a moaning, groaning, dying patient who was disturbing the whole floor, the doctor arranged for him to be transferred to a convalescent home (for those who won't ever convalesce again). But my Dad's bride of seven years, insisted that he be moved instead to their little single apartment, which they called home. He was carried home. My angelic stepmother nursed him day and night, and two weeks later he walked unsteadily with a cane—and one week later, he tossed the cane away. And the reason he is alive and well as of this writing is because he had a home to come back to, and a companion who cared. (And he told me he'll be damned if he'll go, until he sees a copy of this book.)

And not incidentally, my Dad still has his bank account (shrunken because of his hospitalization); his Social Security checks; no pot belly (shrunken because of lovingly supervised diet cooking); no more hacking cough (because no more cigarettes); I'm not sure about the prostate (I'm embarrassed to ask the bridegroom even though I know him well), but I know he still has his bushy head of hair.

CHAPTER XV

AGE DISCRIMINATION

or living in an age of stupidity

The erosion of the individual's rights by the nine omnipotent prophets called the Supreme Court, is best exemplified by my recent experiences.

As mentioned earlier, my wife requires assistance since she does not have the use of her left arm and she walks with difficulty with a quad cane. So when our live-in companion/ homemaker decided to take an extended trip, we were once again in the market for a replacement.

I applied to the Department of Employment as I was under the impression that many people are unemployed. (I was corrected and told that its new name was Department for the Development of Human Resources. It should have been

called Agency for the Waste of Human Resources.) I was referred to the Job Bank, and immediately informed that this
was a tough assignment, the most difficult of all to fill. I
was puzzled. Thousands of unemployed women but no
homemakers?

I gave my requirements as "Mature woman over age 50"
—the interviewer cut in, "Sorry, you can't say over 50. That
is discriminatory." I then asked, "How about over age 60? I
certainly cannot be accused of discrimination against older
people. You passed this law to protect the older people."

"Sorry, you can't say over 50 or over 60. That is not
allowed, but we can say over 40." I gasped, "How can you
say 40 is not discriminatory, but 50 or 60 is?"

"Don't know. But we are allowed to say over 40, according to the rules of this department."

Stupid! I have proved stupidity—right?

So I was listed by the Job Bank—and they were right. I
did not receive a single inquiry within three weeks from the
Department for the Development of Human Resources.

Next I phoned a newspaper to place an ad in their classified section. As I began to read my ad—"Mature unencumbered lady. . . ." I was interrupted, "Sorry, you cannot say
'lady'—it is against the law." I couldn't believe it. "But I want
a lady to assist my wife get dressed, bathed, etc." "Sorry, we
cannot accept the ad if it specifies sex. You can say—mature
unencumbered *person.*"

"O.K., I've got to advertise, but I'll be damned if I'll
interview any man who answers."

"That's up to you, but you know that if you refuse to
interview a man because of sex, he can sue you."

My dear readers—I assure you that I will never interview any male for this job and he can sue. I'll gladly fight this case all the way, because I am willing to fight for my rights which our idiotic society has taken from me!

And for your information—we actually got six male applicants, all of whom I challenged and only one gave me any argument when I said no man was going to dress and bathe my wife. The one who argued stated that he was gay and therefore he saw no reason for my refusal. He too can sue!

Unbelievable what our political wise men will do to buy the votes of any organized pressure group.

What has this to do with retirement? Plenty! For my definition of retirement is to be actively working, be productive, be of service—not vegetating. And as the Job Bank will tell you, there are thousands of openings for homemakers, but no applicants. Why? Because our government agencies have decided such work is degrading.

F.N. didn't think so.

PROFILE OF F.N.

At age 51—a displaced homemaker.

F.N.'s husband worked for a large engineering company with contracts all over the world. He was often away from home on foreign assignments. The money was good and F.N. didn't have to work, so she didn't. But she once figured out that they actually lived together only 12 years, four months, and 102 days, although they were married 29 years. She said, "He never got an assignment in Paris, London, or Rome. It was always a place where there were no modern toilet facilities—and since I wasn't cut out for roughing it, I kept the light shining in the window in Omaha."

Yet, it was a congenial marriage, for they had more honey-
moons than ZaZa.

F.N. was 51 when her husband passed away. To her surprise, a well-off wife is not necessarily a financially secure
widow. She had a survivor pension of $423 a month from
the company; an expensive all-paid-for car; expensive all-
paid-for furniture; and some money but not enough to live
off the interest. So she had to go to work. Waitressing was
the only job easily procurable at her age. The money was
pretty good but those deductions—and the rent for the
apartment—and food—and the utilities—there wasn't too
much left. And as the years passed, she realized that her
legs might not hold up. So she began to worry about five,
ten or more years from now.

One of her closest friends was a widow who had been left
practically penniless, with no pension—and who had to give
up her apartment and take a live-in job caring for an elderly
gentleman. She compared notes with her friend (and expenses) and found that her friend had a better net take-
home pay than she did earning over twice as much. Plus
more security and less wear and tear on the legs.

For the past two years, F.N. (now 55) has been the live-in
homemaker for an older couple.

RATING BY J.S.: Perfect example of a displaced homemaker becoming a productive whole person.

For there is no more noble profession than the making
a house a home.

* * * * * * * * * * * * * *

Thousands of displaced homemakers need these jobs,
but our Welfare Society has created a Cheating Society. During the past ten years, I have interviewed over 100 women
for a homemaker's position. Over 75% would have accepted

the job PROVIDED I paid them in cash and *not pay* Social
Security tax on their earnings (as the law requires me to do).
They were either drawing disability benefits, unemployment,
welfare, food stamps, supplemental income, etc., and they
were by no means members of any minority group—the
largest number by far, were white native-born Americans.

Many told me they wished they could try the job for a
trial period, but they were fearful that once they got off the
welfare rolls, it might be months before they could get back
on. I could not engage them for a trial period without dis-
closure, and they could not work for pay (they said) without
losing their place in the welfare line. I was sorry for those
women and angry at our incentiveless welfare system.

But I do not have any sympathy for the others who
brazenly boasted that they always worked and received un-
reported wages while they continued to collect welfare.

I accuse our government and our legislators as aiding in
the deterioration of morality and honesty through welfare
rules that make decent citizens into scofflaws.

* * * * * * * * * * * * * *

And the profusion of anti-discrimination laws are a joke
(but it ain't funny) for no one discriminates more than our
own government.

PROOF: A few years ago, I drove our homemaker to
the Social Security office. She was soon to be 62 years of age
and she (in accordance with my philosophy) wished to apply
for retirement benefits to begin as of 62. After I waited in
the car for an hour, I went into the office and found she was
still waiting to be called for an interview. I approached the
reception desk and asked the girl how long it might be before
my friend was called and she said,

"Sorry, but it may still be some time because we are terribly understaffed—in fact we are also interviewing applicants for jobs with our department so that we can give better service."

I was interested, since I had eleven years experience in pension planning and I was soon to retire (to go to work) so I said,

"Whom can I see about discussing a job with this Department?" She hesitantly answered, "Well I really don't think you—you—I don't think you will be eligible."

This made me angry—I asked, "Why, am I too old?"

She, fumbling for words, "Well—that's part of it, I guess."

"Young lady—you cannot turn me down because of age. That is your rule against age discrimination. So now I insist, whom do I see about a job?"

A few minutes later, I was seated in front of the manager's desk. After telling him my qualifications, he forthrightly said,

"You are eminently qualified, in fact I am sure you could handle my job. I would love to have you with us and if you insist, I will certainly give you an application. But there is no sense in my kidding you. Your application will never be reviewed. It will be pigeonholed and you will never even be notified that you are not acceptable."

"Because of my age?"

"No, not your age. It's the color of your skin, and the lack of a foreign accent."

"You must be kidding. How can the government condone reverse discrimination?"

"Easy—by a memo regarding the hiring of new employees. We are *not told* we cannot hire a white native-born, but we are told that we must hire people with Spanish surnames, or blacks."

CHAPTER XVI

MANDATORY RETIREMENT AT AGE 65 OR 70

much ado about nothing

The abolishment of mandatory retirement at age 65, and moving it up to age 70, is an example of legislated nonsense. In 1977, it blossomed into a front page crusade with John Wayne, Ruth Gordon, and Will Geer, as the stars at a hearing in Washington. At the risk of offending many sincere people, including the AARP, the Gray Panthers, Senator Claude Pepper and John Wayne, I maintain that they solved a small problem, affecting only a few people, AND INSTEAD created a much larger problem for most of the people.

Before we leave the movie star proponents, I ask you, "How relevant is their testimony attacking mandatory retirement? Do movie stars, or playwrights, or artists, or symphony conductors have to retire at 65? They never did, and they never will."

* * * * * * * * * * * * * *

What is (or was) the meaning of mandatory retirement? It was a company policy established by many major employers that their employees retire when they reached a certain age, usually 65. The employees had 20, 30 or 40 years advance notice, according to their age at beginning of employment.

Labor unions for many years, not only endorsed mandatory retirement, but also encouraged earlier retirement by negotiating pensions to begin at ages earlier than 65. Orderly advancement opportunities for younger employees and spreading employment to more of our population, were major objectives of the mandatory retirement policy. And you will note, that labor unions took no position in the 1977 campaign to outlaw such a policy.

The vast majority prefer *earlier* retirement, *not later.* Federal workers are retiring earlier than ever before. In 1965, the average retirement age of government employees was 64.1 years. In 1976, it had dropped to 61.1 years, but the average of all those retiring in 1976, was 58.2 years. Does this indicate a desire, or a need, to allow Federal workers to stay on the job *beyond age 70?*

At Chrysler Corporation, the mandatory age was 68, but less than 1% remained until 68, for they retired between 55 to 60. At Illinois Bell, the average age of the retirees has been 61 years. Does this indicate a desire, or a need, to force those companies to allow their employeeᵤ to remain on thᵤ job *until age 70?*

Of course, there will always be some employees whᵤ won't want to quit, at any age. But only a very few. According to one survey (admitted by the proponents) only 7% of those about to retire, indicated that they might have considered continuing on the job, if allowed to. So 93% were sure they wanted to retire.

Yet it was claimed that mandatory retirement was a form of age discrimination, and they sounded off as though the majority did not want to quit, at any age. Then how is it, that over 50% of our seniors drawing Social Security retirement benefits, applied for their benefits EARLY—BEFORE AGE 65?

It's the same old story. A loud minority with the magic word DISCRIMINATION, can make Congress move with unusual harmony and speed, to right a wrong.

Let us see how Congress solved this so-called wrong. They outlawed mandatory retirement at age 65—and raised it to age 70. This was applicable to the private sector. For their own federal employees, they were much more expansive (and expensive). Federal employees are no longer subject to an age 70 mandatory retirement age—they can work at their jobs FOREVER. (I am confused. The same Congress just a few months earlier, passed a law forcing federal law enforcement officers to quit at age 55. So FBI agent, Edward Armbruster, had to retire in December 1977—at age 85.)

What did Congress actually accomplish? Our nation would have been better served if they had gone the other way, and forced mandatory retirement at 55, for all. (I mean —my kind of retirement—to change to other work.)

Age discrimination has not been alleviated by this new law. Congress is now a party to *increased* age discrimination. But this time it is against our younger aged population.

We have too many laws on the books. Anyone's gripe that can be cloaked with the suspicion of discrimination, is a prime target for any cause-group to form another national do-good organization. And they have legislators knocking at their door, asking for the privilege of sponsoring their anti-discrimination bill—and appearing as the dinner speaker at their national convention. For legislators must legislate, otherwise, they have no work for their staffs.

Although many of the advocates for this absurd law were attracted by its social aspect, for some it was a personal vendetta—although they always pointed to others. Anyone can find one man or woman, whose umbilical cord was cut by the 65 mandatory rule, and who is shouting loud and clear, "It ain't fair." But the same shouting by the same person will be heard at age 70.

Isn't 20, 30 or 40 years enough advance notice?

Mrs. B.L. didn't think 60 years was enough advance notice.

PROFILE OF B.L.

Retired at age 82 and wife is angry.

B.L. was 22 when he started—and when he reached 65, no one had the nerve to tell him to retire. So he stayed on until he reached 70. The company gave him a 70th birthday party and a new TV set, so he must have known this was a retirement party. But B.L. is hard of hearing, and he was at his desk the next morning. Some of the old time customers got into the spirit of the game and they would call for B.L. to take their orders. But time takes its toll, and they didn't last as long as B.L.

He came to work even though he no longer drove his car. His young wife (1 year younger) now drove him and picked him up each night. This went on for 12 more years. And when B.L. reached 82, the boss finally got up the courage to tell him that someone else was going to take over his desk.

B.L. is a good sport about it, but his wife is furious. She told me, "The idea of firing a man of 82. Where is he supposed to get a new job at his age?" I ventured with, "Why should he look for another job? You've got enough money without his working." She hit me with, "A man doesn't belong in the house. He can work. I don't want him under my feet at home. And I know you Schwartz, you want people to retire early and give their jobs to young people.

Let them find their own jobs. This one was my husband's. And I want him to sue for age discrimination, but he won't do it."

RATING BY J.S.: I would not have believed it either, if I hadn't heard it.

B.L. is still active and helping out at community projects, according to his wife (and verified by me). So what's the problem? Obviously not the loss of the job. Obviously it is the wife. In fact, I wonder—I'll bet B.L. would have retired earlier, but his wife wouldn't let him.

* * * * * * * * * * * * *

Editor to J.S.: Delete B.L. profile as it is too unusual—not typical. Or else, suggest you find and use younger person to make it believable.

J.S. to Editor: I did use a younger person. I have documentation of a man age 90, who in November 1978 sued to get his job back on grounds of age discrimination. I felt that might be considered too unusual.

* * * * * * * * * * * * *

Of course Congress says an employer can get rid of an employee before age 70, if he can prove the employee can no longer perform his duties satisfactorily. Can you visualize the problems facing the employer in such a case—and the expense, both in time and money—and don't forget the delay, the paper work, and the lawyer's fee.

And what happens if an employer has to permanently lay off some workers due to lack of work, and some of them are 65 and can go on pension, and others are young family supporting men and women? Can he lay off the 65 year old?

(In 1978, a new right was proposed. Women are NOT to be fired because of pregnancy—and employers are NOT to refuse to hire a woman because of her pregnant condition.)

Do you realize that the employer is always guilty until proven innocent? An employee who makes a complaint of age discrimination against his employer DOES NOT have to prove his charge—the employer must prove it is not age discrimination.

Humaneness, goodness, and fairness, are NOT exclusively attributable to employees. There are many employers, who are also endowed with such traits. Companies have, and always will have, some long term employees who are not performing the full functions of their jobs, but who are allowed to hang on until mandatory age. Moving the age up to 70 (and soon forever) will force employers to fire some 60's for inability to perform, when they might otherwise have allowed them to hang on until 65. Wait until that hits the fan!

Question: Do you suppose our legislators had something else in mind?

If people held on to their jobs until 70—everyone that does
    1. he will not draw his Social Security until 70
    2. he will continue to pay into the S.S. fund
    3. the S.S. fund does need the money.

No, I don't think those were the reasons for this stupid law, because they would have said so—wouldn't they?

To prove that I do not condemn all actions of our lawmakers:

A door-to-door salesman in Los Angeles, complained that he was deprived of his rights, in that the gas stations did not provide restroom facilities for the *non-customer pedestrian.* So he got his cause before the L.A. City Council. The Council was faced with passing a law to force all gas stations, restaurants, etc., to provide restroom facilities for the public at large.

To the credit of the political hierarchy, it was rejected by a vote of 13 to 0.

NOTE: Someone must have alerted the City Council, that if it was approved, it would be discriminatory, unless it included all private homes. And why stop at toilet accommodations? Why not provide showers—and don't forget the towels.

* * * * * * * * * * * * * *

Dear Reader:

The Los Angeles incident reported above, actually happened. It is *no* joke.

The new law changing mandatory retirement from age 65 to age 70 also actually happened. It *is* a joke.

J.S.

CHAPTER XVII

THE SINGLE HOME AND THE SENIOR
can you afford to live in your own home?

To my grandparents and my parents, ownership of a house was the foundation of their older age planning. To them, the ownership of one's own home was the ultimate in security. It was a roof over one's head—NOT FOR SALE, for it was home, to be passed on to the next generation.

To my children's and grandchildren's generations, the ownership of a single house; a condominium; a cooperative apartment; or an apartment building will be the beginning of their retirement financial planning. To these younger generations, afflicted, infected, and having accepted inflation as a way of life, ownership means an inflationary investment—FOR SALE or exchange—for money.

Somewhere, sometime between these family generation eras, the concept of ownership of a home has changed considerably. Let's see how this affects my generation, you, and you, and you, and me.

* * * * * * * * * * * * * *

The most expensive form of housing today is the single home. It wasn't always so, for ownership used to be the cheapest form of housing. Today because of inflation and a shortage of housing, single homes command outrageously high prices. Yet the propaganda continues that every person in our affluent society should aspire to owning his own home. The media and the politician call it the American dream. At the risk of being called unpatriotic, I suggest that there is a time for owning your home, and a time for selling.

The retired homeowner who is in need of additional retirement income should give the question of selling serious consideration. Do you still have need for three bedrooms, two baths, large lawn and backyard now that the children are gone? A single home could be justified as a necessity when the family needed growing-up space and when you were earning full-time wages. But when faced with the certainty of a sizable reduction in income, it is indisputable that you should get rid of your Rolls Royce and get a Chevy.

A retiree who has owned his home for a number of years, will find that selling his home is the easiest way to increase his income. Yes, even if it is completely paid-for and the taxes are only $100 a month, and even though any suitable apartment would cost $300 a month or more. I've heard these words time and time again: "My house is paid-up and I will stay here for the rest of my life because my taxes are much less than the cost of an apartment." If this is your position, then your arithmetic may be wrong.

Because of the strange American sanctification of home and the acceptance that we will always have inflation, special income tax forgiveness have been allowed all homeowners when they sell their homes. Due to the growing political strength of old agers, extra-special income tax benefits have been bestowed on senior citizen homeowners when they sell. Homeowners have become an elite privileged class, and senior homeowners are nobility to whom all others must *pay* homage. Wait until the renters wake up and start screaming for equal rights. You won't have to wait very long.

For the past few years, all homeowners of ANY AGE have been permitted to sell their residence with no tax payable on any profit PROVIDED they purchased or built another home (within a specified period) costing as much or more than the home they sold. This is commonly referred to as a rollover privilege.

Seniors OVER AGE 65 who sold their homes were allowed a special tax concession even though they did not rollover. If the net sales price was $35,000 or less, the entire profit was theirs to keep without tax; if more than $35,000, only part of the profit was tax-free based on a specific formula. I never could understand the justification of a tax reduction for a seller over age 65, but not if age 64. Don't bother trying to figure it out—it has been changed to age 55 BUT NOT 54, and it has been rasied to $100,000.

In 1978, California, in a knee-jerk reaction to its famous Proposition 13 property tax revolt, granted home-sellers OF ANY AGE (a once in a lifetime) up to $100,000 profit TAX-FREE. And Congress was not far behind as they hastened to join the tax-reduction movement by also voting a once-in-a lifetime $100,000 tax-free profit. But since this special privilege is difficult to justify, and to make it known that they do not blindly follow a lowly state's lead, Washington restricted this bonanza to home-sellers age 55 and older.

This restriction makes it appear to be an old age benefit—which needs no justification.*

The rollover privilege allows families to avoid all capital-gains taxes on home profits thoughout their lifetime, even though they buy homes and sell homes, and buy again and sell again, and again and again. And finally when age 55 has happily been reached, they can sell their last inflated home and keep $100,000 profit tax-free.

So a home is the ultimate in the tax shelter field, for $100,000 profit is tax exempt. Where this will end, no one knows, but the trend is firmly established. Your government proclaims that the purchase of a home is the way for every American to take advantage of inflation, but they forget to warn you that you are sure of a profit ONLY AS LONG AS THE HOUSING SHORTAGE CONTINUES.

Some people reason that the elected officials are giving senior citizens tax breaks in order that they will sell their homes to the young who are blaming government for the house shortage. I do not believe that is the reason but I do agree that will be the result. For it certainly is an incentive to sell.

* * * * * * * * * * * * * *

If you are a low-income or middle-income retiree and you can sell your home for a sizable profit—can you afford to live in your own home AFTER AGE 55?

If you can sell at a profit of $100,000 and you invest it in a savings and loan long term certificate @ 8.33% annual interest, you will receive $8333 each year, and you no longer pay property taxes (which I will assume were $1200 annually).

*Check with accountant or IRS for current information *before* selling.

If you move into an apartment for $300, $400 or $500 monthly rental, you have increased your retirement monthly income by almost $500, $400 or $300, plus the security of a $100,000 nest egg. There will be a tax obligation on the interest you receive—but this is somewhat offset by the savings of maintenance costs ordinarily spent in the upkeep of a house.

I must warn you that at this point many financial advisors will disagree with me. They will say that your frozen $100,000 certificate will be worth less each year because of inflationary erosion, whereas your house will be worth more because of inflationary appreciation.

My answer is that if you need more retirement income NOW, then NOW is the time to sell. Inflation cannot continue forever, and neither will your home continue to increase in value forever. *In the 1960's you couldn't sell your home for as much as you had paid for it in the 1950's.* (It will happen again.)

The main reason for the extraordinary inflated value of your home TODAY is that there is a shortage of new homes and a tremendous demand due to the public's acceptance of perpetual inflation. This demand will gain in intensity because of the age 55 $100,000 homeseller tax incentive. And the demand will force a relaxation of environmental and density restrictions, enabling building contractors to construct *more* houses *faster,* so that I predict, in five to ten years the old homes will sell for much less than today due to competition from new homes and condominiums.

It is inevitable that the single home market will be overbuilt. The only question is when?

Some will argue that since building costs will continue to increase, the new houses must continue to command higher prices so the older homes will also continue to increase in value. But rows upon rows of newly built VACANT houses and condominiums, and bankruptcies of over-extended builders, will have a depressing effect on prices. THERE IS NO SUCH THING AS A SURE THING—FOREVER!

I dare say this despite the financial inflation experts' predictions that homes that are selling for $100,000 today, will in ten years be selling for $250,000. I say, our economy cannot survive another ten years with continuing rampant inflation. It will be stopped or we will have a complete collapse of our individual and national security.

So as the old-time carnival barker used to say, "Put up your money and take your choice. Under which shell will we find the pea? If you guess right, you win. If not, you lose."

It's your money and your choice. You find the pea.

* * * * * * * * * * * * * *

If you have never lived in an apartment, this will be a new experience—like Listerine, you'll either love it, or hate it. There are many pluses to apartment living, not the least of which is the freedom to move if you don't care for your common wall or top of your ceiling neighbors. But the common wall is also a plus, because the security of having neighbors on the other side of the lathe and plaster is of major importance.

If you are living alone it is even more important, for there is less crime committed against apartment dwellers than against occupants in individual homes. For reasons of security, older folks should consider apartment life.

If I sound as though I am pro-apartments, I no doubt am. For I preach what I practice. I own an apartment building in which I live. This I recommend as being one of the best solutions to a retired person's housing problem. It also solves the problem of boredom by providing a meaningful and sociable activity.

Shortly after I retired for my first time, I put into writing my impression of apartment buildings as investments for retirees. Following is a condensed version of my experience.

* * * * * * * * * * * * *

When I traded our home towards a 15 unit apartment building, I did not realize that this would introduce me to a new career. I never gave any consideration to the maligned business of owning and operating apartment buildings. To me it was just an investment, but I soon discovered it was a new career—exciting, profitable, and essential—meeting an important social need.

But please understand, that ownership alone does not earn the superlatives that I have attributed to the apartment business. It also requires proper operation which includes a deep consideration for your tenant customers.

Ownership is simple, for anyone with money can be an owner. But the operation of the building is much more exacting and rewarding. With proper operation, the owner has a fool-proof investment, better than gold, silver, or the collection of fine arts, to weather the constant erosion caused by inflation—and to ride out the turbulence of the depression which will one day mark the end of inflation.

There is no better way for a retiree to hedge against today's inflation, for the value and net income of apartment buildings increase, as taxes, plumbing, labor increase. And even more important, there are those who, like me, discover this to be an exciting career to retire to. Sure, it will cause you to have problems, aggravations, and worries, such as a thinking human being should expect—but you will be an active, contributing member of society; you will enjoy solving the problems, eliminating the aggravations, and replacing the worries with accomplishments.

A person of any age might consider the ownership of an apartment building as a long or short term investment, devoting little time with little involvement in its operation. But if you are retired or soon-to-retire, you should consider it both as a long term investment and a new career; for you have the time to be involved with tenants, and your time is a good reason for your involvement.

For the majority who need or wish to have additional retirement income, the answer is here—go into business for yourself. The earnings from the apartment business is investment income, and has NO EFFECT whatever on your right to collect Social Security retirement benefits.

For the retired executive accustomed to running the show and making decisions, the ownership/operation of apartment buildings can be the fulfillment of his lifetime career, for now he can be the sole 100% stockholder, with no Board of Directors to appease. He will make a marvelous landlord for he is accustomed to spending money to maintain equipment and property.

So I advise any spouse of an ex-executive whose marriage is floundering because the "ex-ex" has no one else to boss—buy him an apartment building for Christmas, and he'll get off your back and get back on his feet.

But no matter what your age and circumstance, if you are seeking a second career with an opportunity for profit, and with as much, or as little, involvement as you yourself decide—then consider becoming the owner of one or more apartment buildings. And purchase one that you would be willing to live in yourself, because if you wish to reduce your housing expenses after retirement—that is the best way to go.

* * * * * * * * * * * * * * *

I realize that there are many people who love their home and who would be emotionally upset at the thought of giving up and moving from the house in which they have lived for many years. If you have no financial problems, the luxury of your own private home is certainly yours to enjoy. However if you must reduce expenses and you desperately wish to hold on to your old homestead, I recommend that you share your home (or too expensive apartment) with a home-sharer (a roomer who shares the entire home). Look for a friend or a relative that might be faced with the same financial problem. Your church or fraternal organization is also a good source.

Home-sharing has become so popular that there are private agencies in most cities called "Roommate Finders" (or similar names) who assist in finding both roomers and home-sharers. They recognize that such a service is especially applicable to the older age group, and the reputable agency makes every effort to screen for compatibility. But never, and I mean NEVER, allow anyone to move into your home without your having checked their references and being absolutely satisfied that you would be pleased to have them as a member of your family. For you are not only going to reduce your expenses but also reduce your privacy. Many singles have doubled up and this is a good trend, for I am a firm believer that "Man was not meant to live alone."

Everything said about the expense of maintaining a single home is also applicable to condominiums. However a condominium does offer increased security, just as an apartment building, for there is less crime against condominium complex residents than against people living in isolated single homes.

CHAPTER XVIII

RETIREMENT COMMUNITIES
disneyland for seniors

Writers on the subject of retirement communities differ greatly. Some endorse them enthusiastically, and to others they are a form of ghetto. Some say it is bad to be surrounded by the old, the sick, and the "waiting to die people." But others say it is good to live among your contemporaries where everyone is understanding of their common problems. Some praise the security of the stone walls as keeping the outsiders out, while other claim the walls are keeping the insiders in. So some praise, some criticize, and some condemn— and I am in full agreement with all of them.

The larger private-for-profit retirement complexes such as Leisure World and Sun City are not inexpensive, so they appeal to the middle and upper income seniors. Their advertising brochures invite you to investigate, which you should, if at all interested. They have a waiting list of applicants as a rule, which proves the obvious, that senior citizens are not the least affluent segment of our society.

At Leisure World, Laguna Hills, California, a lottery was held in 1977. The winning number meant that a senior had his choice of one of 193 new homes selling for $43,900 to $99,999. They were all sold, many for cash, and there is an ever increasing waiting list, as evidenced by the next lottery held only a few months later. This time it was for 240 homes not yet built, to be ready for occupancy one year later. And this time the prices ranged from $73,400 to $134,900.

The wealth of knowledge concentrated in Leisure World, staggers the imagination. Physicians, philosophers, mathematicians, judges, educators, historians, economists, business executives—men and women of national and world-wide fame, live, play, and work here.

We have all heard that our federal government has ultra-secret bombproof shelters for our President, Cabinet officers, etc., in the event of a nuclear attack. I propose that such shelters be provided for the residents of Leisure World, because if our entire population were annihilated, but our Leisure World inhabitants were the sole survivors, we would have the capacity of re-establishing a better world. (Perhaps cloning is more fun, anyway.)

Why does one common locale such as Leisure World, Laguna Hills, California, appeal to seniors who have so many different interests?

I am ashamed to admit that (in our land of *law and order*) the most important common reason is the search for personal security. What is the worth of peace of mind, provided by a five foot concrete wall, with barbed wire on all exposed areas? And how do you evaluate the worth of being

able to safely walk the streets, and go to sleep with your win-
dows open—knowing that you are protected by a private
police force of over 200 security guards? (Not co-incidentally
many of the guards are retiree residents, who are earning
enough, but not too much to interfere with their Social
Security.)

There are also many other more pleasant reasons (otherwise, San Quentin could qualify as a retirement community).
No lawns to water or trim, because the community sprinkler
system extends to every blade of grass, and there are about
200 full-time gardeners to manicure every lawn. All homes
are not only kept-up landscape wise, but they are painted
every few years whether the exterior is faded or not. Free
community bus service transporting residents to shopping
centers, churches, and banks. A closed circuit TV channel
and their own weekly newspaper, which are essential to list
the community and club functions, for they have over 200
fraternal and social clubs, from Kiwanis to bridge. There is
a club for every profession or interest—attorneys, physicians,
gardening, stamp collecting, music, etc.

It all adds up to one of the most exhilerating, exciting,
cultural cities in all the world. Because its 20,000 residents
are all mature senior citizens, who came here to live—not to
retire.

* * * * * * * * * * * * * *

The plush Leisure World type of retirement community
is obviously not typical. Retirement communities come in all
sizes, styles, and prices—from single homes, to high-rise buildings, to mobile parks. Many provide some of the social activ-
ites of a Leisure World, but on a less lavish scale. Some are
government subsidized, church projects, fraternal supported,
and all of these understandably also have a large waiting list
of applicants. For those in financial need, the subsidized

complexes, are, indeed a blessing. There are so many, both private and public funded, all different in facilities and in entrance requirements, that it is impossible to generalize. And those that require a prospective retiree to sign over all, or most, of his assets, should be investigated thoroughly and hesitantly—yes, even if his church is the sponsor.

But, unfortunately, the retirement community total impact on needy senior citizen housing, is, and always will be, most insignificant.

* * * * * * * * * * * * * *

If you are contemplating life in a walled-in retirement community, consider the following:

If you must supplement your income with part-time work, a retirement community is not for you, for it is not in the main stream of work opportunity.

If you are a widow and hope to remarry, a retirement complex is not a good market place, for they are already over-populated with widows.

If you are a widower and hope to remarry, a retirement community is an excellent shopping place. It is a buyer's market for the single male, no matter how old. In fact, don't bother buying or moving in—just arrange to visit and let it be known that you are available. (And if you got the idea from this book, you should at least invite me to the wedding.)

If you are a senior couple, you will be in the upper social strata, the envy of all singles, for couples will be a minority in any R.C.

If you are a happy, busy, retired couple like Mr. and Mrs. N.E.—You will enjoy R.C. life—and you live it fully.

PROFILE OF N.E.

Retired at 55—12 years ago.

N.E. was a partner and officer in a small successful manufacturing plant which was taken over by a national company on an exchange of stock basis. Having been an owner/boss, N.E. was not happy with his loss of independence, so he quit at age 55. He had no money problems.

He and his wife have enjoyed their retired mode of life, since he keeps very busy with his hobbies and she is busy with hers—and many of their interests are mutual. He enjoys philatelics and has become very proficient in an unusual form of art using stamps in montage and portrait designs. He and his wife love plants and flowers and attend many lectures and flower shows. He also studies and is involved in many investment projects.

They claim that everyone owes some of his time to society. So he works with small business under SCORE, and she is a volunteer worker at a rest home for the aged.

No golf, tennis, or boating. People, things that grow, and an appreciation of the arts enable this couple to enjoy every day of their life.

They are seriously considering moving to a Leisure World or Sun City retirement community. If they do, they will be among the leaders of the study and educational activities.

RATING BY J.S.: Happy, content and living a useful busy retired life. If they have any aches or pains—no one will ever know—for they only share the good.

* * * * * * * * * * * * * *

Senior couples and singles who enjoy group activities and who have always participated in their church and club functions, will find retirement communal living to be to their liking. It can be an ocean voyage on land, all fun and games. Although the majority will sing its praises, some are sure to tire of leisure fun life and their R.C. home will be for sale (for a higher price, if present experience continues).

However, retirement communities will never be housing the majority of our Senior Citizens, because the majority of our older people are not the moving up-rooting type—they are stay-putters.

People have a natural inclination to wish to continue to live in the same community in which they spent their work-ing, family-bringing-up years. Many will sell their empty nest as it becomes too large and too expensive to maintain— but they will be more apt to stay in town rather than pull up stakes. So I predict a constant growth of suburbia retirement clusters on the outskirts of town, appealing to the residents of that town rather than out-of-towners. And I make this pre-diction knowing full well that the winters in New Hampshire can be cold and snow bound.

To be inconsistent, I also admit that our warmer tropi-cal states such as Florida and California will always be an attraction to many out-of-towners. In fact, the largest retire-ment community in the country is Miami Beach. It has everything that any R.C. has except that it is ungated and unwalled. I'm not downing it. I think it's great, especially for the less affluent. Although it has many well-to-do resi-dents and seasonal visitors, and world renowned lavish hotels, apartments, and condominiums, it is also a haven for thou-sands of tightly budgeted Social Securitants, and even fugi-tives from nursing homes. It is the poor man's leisure world, but don't try it without money. Miami Beach landlords and hotel owners also have discovered how to eliminate watering and trimming the lawn. They dug it up, cemented it over, and placed thousands of rocking chairs on reclaimed porches and terraces.

California has its own miniature Miami Beach it calls Venice, a suburban retirement cluster on the outskirts of Los Angeles. Santa Monica, California, has Lawrence Welk and his Senior Citizen high-rise. And though Californians think all of Iowa has moved into Long Beach, and Arizonians know all retirees are heading their way, I still maintain that the majority of older folks prefer and will continue to prefer staying home.

CHAPTER XIX

MOBILE HOMES

retirement community parking lots

Because of Lois, I became acquainted with another planet on this earth called the Mobile Park. And because of me, Lois is now the proud owner of a mobile home. Until this occurred, I knew nothing about this subject, in fact, I had never been inside one of those "tin boxes." But now I am an expert and would not hesitate to purchase one as my home. I am convinced that dollar for dollar, the mobile home is by far the best buy as a permanent residence.

Lois was a dedicated, most compassionate, registered nurse. She also raised, fed, nursed, and educated five children—all members of one family who lost their parents and were faced with the inevitability of being split up. Lois picks up and cares for stray dogs, so it was no surprise that she took this brood over as her own, and did not let go until they were all grown up and on their own. She knew she would not need a large house after the children were grown up, whereas she did need money for their college expenses. So she sold her home. Mission accomplished, all five are now raising their own families, and it is a tribute to their loving upbringing, that they in turn are all together living in the same city, although it is 2000 miles from their foster mother.

After many years of hospital duty, Lois was hospitalized, came out with only one lung, and retired. When Lois took ill, she had been living in a modest apartment for a number of years. One day the building was sold and Lois was given a 60 day notice to move.

Although Lois was ill, she was not financially insecure for she had prudently saved for a rainy day. Her Social Security and hospital pension income was sufficient for her modest needs and she had a sizable savings account balance of $23,000. So she decided she wanted the security of her own home to live for the rest of her life without the fear of rent increases and threat of eviction.

She had used up half of her 60 day notice when she phoned me. She was distraught after 30 days of looking at houses that were not only over-priced but also run-down and in slum areas, for she was in the market to purchase a home for cash, not to exceed $20,000. And it had to be on flat terrain so she could walk to a bus, for she had no car and was unable to walk more than a short block without gasping for air.

When I took control, I told her that her worries were over as I would find a house within her means. After many miles on my speedometer and a whole week of day and night searching, in areas that I had never before traversed, I gave up. Houses close to bus lines and supermarkets in middle class areas were at a premium. Those she could afford could only be found in isolated rural areas.

By now Lois was looking at houses in the 35 to $40,000 class, which she could neither afford nor finance through any conventional mortgage company, for she was disabled and unemployed, and her income would not qualify her for a mortgage.

In desperation, because this was a challenge to the theme of this book, I researched every form of retirement housing. I found a field I had never explored, the mobile home. Naturally I was aware that there were campers, motor homes, and mobile homes. The ads promised that they were low cost housing.

I learned that there was a marked difference in their purposes. Campers and motor homes are most adaptable for the active foot-loose mobile person, whereas mobile homes are not really mobile. They are affixed permanently on a floor (concrete slab) in a residential area and in a variety of locations ranging from slums to beautiful lake front and golf course settings. If one day you decide you don't like your neighbors or your location, the mobile home is mobile to the extent that you can move it to another slab or pad.

So I went to a dealer's display of mobile homes. And when I stepped into those tin boxes I was amazed at the beauty, efficiency, comfort, convenience and low price when assessed against a comparable conventional house. I found that there were many resales available in various mobile parks. Because of Lois's location needs, plus her two dogs, I was forced to eliminate many otherwise desirable locations. I finally found a middle class, well managed park where a beautiful 60X20 (1200 square feet) seven year old home was for sale for $13,900. It was a Golden West, which was according to my investigation, one of the most reputable builders: with two bedrooms, two bathrooms, modern fully equipped kitchen, paneled throughout, carpeted, draped, large covered patio, and air conditioned.

Lois had never seen the interior of a mobile home. When I drove her to what I had described as "it," I noticed that she became quiet and I could tell that she had her reservations. As we waited for the sales agent to arrive for our interview, I could sense Lois's awful disappointment. I asked her to reserve her decision until she had inspected the interior and assured her she was under no obligation to purchase it merely because I had chosen it.

She admitted to me later that she did not even want to get out of the car and go into the tin box. She was trying to find the words to tell me so, but she couldn't.

The moment we stepped inside, Lois's face brightened. She hurried from one room to the next, positively enthralled. She immediately said, "I want it. I want it. This is it."

I explained that she did not own the land upon which the home was set. She would always have to pay rent, which was $100 a month including all utilities, and the rent could be raised. However a single home of comparable size would have a property tax assessment of at least $80 to $100 a month. I also explained that the mobile home was going to be taxed as a motor vehicle which would cost approximately $100 per year (which also could and would be raised in future years). Nothing could dampen her enthusiasm. "I want it! I want it!"

So Lois is now living in her own home, surrounded by friendly neighbors who have all discovered that mobile home living can be beautiful, and fun, and much less expensive than a single home or condominium.

And I have also learned that many mobile parks are

miniature Leisure Worlds and should be explored by every retired couple or single who wishes to live first class on a second class income.

> NOTE: For a complete list and description of all mobile home parks in your area and throughout the country—see directory published by
> Woodall Publishing Co.
> 500 Hyacinth Place
> Highland Park, Illinois 60035
> (also available in most public libraries)

CHAPTER XX

INFLATION

as long as you like it

I promised to deal with inflation, but remember, I did not promise to solve it (although I have some ideas on this too).

Pre-retirement planning is difficult in the light of what appears to be permanent escalating inflation. Obviously, people on fixed incomes are most affected, therefore our retired population are—and should be—concerned. The trouble is it is not concerned enough to take the action that is needed.

The reason we have inflation, and will continue to have more inflation, is because YOU LIKE IT.

* * * * * * * * * * * * * *

The workers love it, especially union members, for to them inflation promises ever-increasing wages. Keep inflation going, just until the next wage boost—then stop it. That may sound fine in theory until another organized group protests that they haven't gotten their's yet, so keep it going for a little while longer.

The senior citizen loves it and wants it to continue until he has sold his single home.

The junior citizen who bought the house, loves inflation and wants it to continue until he becomes a senior citizen, and sells the house for a much higher price, to another junior citizen.

The farmer wants it to continue until he can get a higher parity (whatever that means)—and when, and if, he gets his cut, he, too, will love it.

The welfare recipient loves it, because it means his allotment must be increased.

The social worker loves it, because it means a larger case load, which means a larger salary, and more social workers.

The Social Security pensioner loves it, for he knows it is responsible for the regular increases in his checks.

Everybody talks *anti*-inflation; everyone gripes about inflation; but they are all chronic liars, because THEY don't want it to stop, at least not before they get theirs.

That doesn't mean that inflation is good. If cancer is good for you, then so is inflation. If not treated in time, both can eat you alive, cancer physically, inflation financially.

So what does our government do about it? Nothing? Unfortunately not. Worse than nothing. While "jawboning" against inflation, they proceed to legislate more of the same.

* * * * * * * * * * * * * *

Your government thrives on inflation. Inflation helps to justify budget and staff increases and gives "civil servants" a lot of busy work KEEPING TRACK OF INFLATION.

Just think of the number of public employees engaged in the non-productive task of computing the percentage increase of inflation every day, week, month and year. Just think OF THE COST of all those press releases, telling us that the cost of living is up this month, this quarter, this year (while we are in the process of licking inflation). In a way it's like the weather forecaster who tells you what the weather was yesterday.

I wish someone would tell me the purpose of the government's advertising that a family of four, earning less than "$16,236.75" is unable to maintain a decent, just moderate, standard of living. Just think of the effect this has on the wage earner who is below that figure, and the effect on his wife AND two kids. Thousands of happy Americans thought they were solvent and eating well. Now all of a sudden they have this vital information they never had before, that Dad is a submarginal failure and should be ashamed of himself for not being dissatisfied.

Instead of bolstering consumer morale and confidence, the government's scorekeeping makes it plunge even lower. Next year, it will publicize an even higher bare subsistence figure for a family of four. Yet anyone of us can find families of four, who are getting along very well on less than the bureaucratic figure. And we can find thousands more that would live in a most luxurious style, if they were raised to that figure. Whose family serves as the comfortably indigent model for the government scorekeepers? Maybe it's Mr. and

Mrs. Scorekeeper themselves, on the scent of a raise. But since no scorekeeper (economist) ever drops below that figure, I fail to see what purpose such figures serve our nation. It can only serve to make more people unhappy and to supply union negotiators with more documented evidence to justify more wage increases to push prices higher and higher.

My major in college was economics. We were taught that prices were controlled by the Law of Supply and Demand. We learned that when large numbers of people were unemployed, prices were depressed. We were told that inflation could not occur in a period of high unemployment. What happened? It appears that the natural economic laws no longer apply. Today's economic laws are shaped by politicians and legislators who see inflation as the simplest means to an end, and keep the Treasury's printing presses going full blast to pay for the binge.

If you don't believe it, try to answer this question: Why do legislators increase the minimum hourly wage in a period of inflation and high unemployment? This only increases the costs of production and creates more unemployment, offsetting most of the wage increases, and creating problems of survival for the fixed income retiree.

At a hearing before the Senate Labor sub-committee in 1977, Labor Secretary F. Ray Marshall admitted that raising the minimum hourly wage to $2.65 could cost 90,000 jobs. The U.S. Chamber of Commerce testified that an increase of 70 cents would cause 700,000 layoffs, and reduce future employment by two million.

So what did Congress do? It passed new minimum hourly wage legislation raising the $2.30 rate to $2.65 effective in 1978; $2.90 in 1979; $3.10 in 1980; and $3.35 in 1981. Congress voted an increase in inflation for four years, and a decrease in employment. How much sense does it make to condemn inflation with one breath and then fan it with another?

The young who are trying to get their first job are the ones who will be most injured by the boosted minimum hourly wage. They are unemployed now, and their chances of getting a job will worsen as the hourly rate increases. Since Congress knows this, how do you explain CETA?

The Comprehensive Employment Training Act (CETA) announced a program designed to create and pay for summer jobs for low-income youths. (Which includes virtually all of youth.) Priority was given to school drop-outs, who were paid the full minimum hourly rate, for from 25 to 40 hours a week, for nine weeks. For most youths, totally inexperienced, green, semiproductive, and in many cases illiterate, this would be their first paying job, at the rate of $100 a week (40 hours). How will these youths feel at the end of nine weeks? Will they ever be satisfied with less than $100 a week? Couldn't some genius in Washington have figured out, that if they were paid $1.50 an hour, there would have been more jobs available, and less dissatisfaction with the outside (of government) industrial world, beginning the tenth week?

This is another glaring example of government inoculating our young with the inflation virus. And to top it off, one of the directors of the program is quoted in a news release as saying, "These jobs are not raking, digging, sweeping type jobs. They are meaningful jobs that give youths a sense of accomplishment and pride." I ask, "What the hell is wrong with raking, digging, and sweeping? Senior citizens have done their share of that type of work—with pride. Why indoctrinate our youth that such work is demeaning?" (Not to mention the hypocrisy of assuming that a totally inexperienced school dropout is by some stretch of the imagination magically qualified to hold a "meaningful" job.)

There is a simple solution to applying the brakes to inflation. It has never been tried, for it might mean political

suicide for the legislator who proposed the SCHWARTZ
DEFLATION FORMULA. I'll tell it to you, and maybe one
Congressman (who is retiring from office) will be brave
enough to introduce it. LOWER THE MINIMUM HOURLY
RATE TO $2.

The result would be lower costs of production, more
new jobs in the private sector, an immediate increase in the
value of the American dollar in the international market, and
everyone would have more purchasing power. This would not
affect the hourly wage of the majority of the working populace, who are earning well over the minimum rate. But it
would give employment to millions of our young, our old,
our poor, and our disadvantaged. And it would help the
fixed-income retirees—for whatever that is worth.

On second thought, it might *not* be political suicide for
the legislator who proposed it—he might, instead, end up in
the White House. For in 1978, *U.S. News & World Report*
sponsored a survey among heads of households, asking them
whether they felt there should be a higher minimum wage IF
IT MEANT MORE UNEMPLOYMENT.
         22% said YES
         68% said NO
         10% were undecided.

So whom do our legislators listen to: the people, or the
union lobbyists?

Inflation will never be stopped, until we get rid of the
Santa Claus philosophy in Washington, your State Capitol,
your City Hall—and the continuous "maximizing" of the
minimum hourly rate.

* * * * * * * * * * * * * *

In the meantime, people on fixed incomes, especially
WE senior retirees, are adversely affected by the constant in-

crease in the cost of our basic needs for living. How do WE cope with it?

We must be much more price conscious and shop smarter.

We should try not only to cope with it, but we should FIGHT IT as well.

We can cause the price of any product to go down, just by invoking the old law of supply and demand. It still can work, if untouched by political hands.

No demand for a product causes a glut in supply, and the price must come down. So, don't buy when the price is high. It's that simple.

Don't buy tomatoes when priced at 89c a pound, and the price will soon come down to 39c. Don't buy coffee when the price is absurd.

If the AARP asked that everyone boycott meat, or fish, or automobiles—within 60 days those products would be of- fered at substantially reduced prices. The government isn't going to do it for us, so we have to do it ourselves. Boycott! Go without coffee for a while and preserve your health as well as your assets. We can drive prices down if we wish. We have the gray power to do it!

* * * * * * * * * * * * * *

But driving down the price of tomatoes and coffee won't solve the whole problem. What is the fixed-income re- tiree to do, *today?*

I never promised that I could tell you how to make

something out of *nothing,* but I can tell you how to make *more* out of *something.*

I admit that the following suggestions are simple, mundane, unoriginal, and already practiced by many, but those of you who do not, should, and you will be surprised at how far those shrinking dollars can be stretched.

1. Don't buy seasonal produce when out of season, and priced out of reason.
2. Don't encourage scalping prices. Boycott obvious rip-offs. Substitute. Or go without.
3. Shop at the day-old bakery outlet stores.
4. Don't buy anything in spray containers if a little dab will do ya. The spray gizmo costs more than the contents.
5. Don't buy your favorite soft drinks in 12 ounce cans. Buy the same root beer in the 32 ounce returnable bottles and you will save 25% to 40%.
6. Pool the costs and exchange the newspapers and magazines you subscribe to with your neighbor. Each of you will reduce paper waste and subscription fees simultaneously.
7. Set up your own gasoline rationing plan. Join a neighborhood car pool for shopping, attending meetings, etc.
8. Continue to observe the energy-saving hints the utilities propose. It will cut your costs and help relieve the energy crunch.
9. Don't trim the lawn or waste money on crabgrass killer. Dig it up and plant a vegetable garden.

The National Association for Gardening claims that an investment of $20, and a few hours each week, produces $300 of vegetables per summer.

10. Join the couponeers. Clipping cents-off coupons saves you dollars and makes good sense.

One person was curious as to the effect coupons had on her grocery bill. So she opened a special bank account in which she deposited the cents-off coupon discounts that she actually received. At the end of one year, she had $1800.
Another mother claimed that due to using discount coupons, she is able to feed her family of seven on a budget of $100 a month.

11. Don't allow yourself to be the victim of planned obsolescence. Hang on to your out-of-style clothes. One of the pluses of being a senior citizen is that you can stop catering to the year-to-year changers. No one will give a damn if your lapels are narrow. Besides, narrow lapels will be in again soon one of these days.

12. Don't ever buy a brand new automobile. Let someone else break it in, get the bugs out, and get walloped with the $1000 to $2000 depreciation just for driving it off the show-room floor.

* * * * * * * * * * * * * * *

I cannot leave the reader thinking that he can cope with inflation for as long as it lasts—for the reader can't last that long. Inflation will destroy us all and must be stopped.

In October 1978 there was a news release that by the year 2050 the average worker will earn $650,000 annually. Doesn't that scare the hell out of you? How much will a loaf of bread cost—$1000?

You're not worried because you figure that you won't be alive in 2050. But what about your children and their children? And how about 1990? You might be alive then, and what will bread cost?

What good is retirement planning? How can anyone plan to live on a fixed income? How can we sit complacently while our government merely reports and condones inflation?

The Tax Revolution will do us no good if INFLATION takes away all of its benefits. We need another people's revolution headed by senior citizens; retirees; all people now on fixed incomes; and all who expect someday to retire on a fixed pension.

CHAPTER XXI

SENIOR CITIZENS
FLEX THEIR MUSCLES

move over — we want it all, too

Let's expose once and for all time the fallacy of the Senior Citizen war cry that "I have been a taxpayer all my life and therefore am entitled to decent housing, ample food, and financial security from the government."

Taxes are supposed to be on a *pay as you go basis.* Instead they are on an *owe as you go basis* or *where did they go?* There aren't any of your taxes left when you get there. If yesterday's taxes did not cover yesterday's public service costs—how in heck do you expect yesterday's taxes to pay for tomorrow's needs?

Your taxes in 1945 went to pay for policemen, firemen, educators, military, elected officials, and public employees salaries, expenses, fringe benefits, etc., *spent in 1945.* Same in 46, 47, 57, 67, 77, etc. In fact, you did not pay enough taxes, since your government spent more than it collected from you. IT and YOU are broke.

The only part of your taxes to which you might have any claim is the Social Security tax (which incidentally also is not enough to pay for the benefits Social Security promises to pay you). So play another tune, Sam. Nobody owes you anything!

But logic doesn't always prevail, especially when voters make demands in a collective voice. And the voice of the Senior Citizen is becoming more vocal for he has discovered the potency of the Senior Citizen organizations.

* * * * * * * * * * * * * *

The American Association of Retired Persons is the largest organized group of retired or about-to-be-retired citizens in this or any other country. Many of my readers are members, and all others have or will receive mail from AARP soliciting them as members. Through AARP, the Senior Citizen is told that he can flex his muscles as a powerful political pressure group.

The American Association of Retired Persons (AARP) owes its existence to a sincere dedicated retired schoolteacher named Ethel Percy Andrus, who created the National Retired Teachers Association (NRTA). Although NRTA is still a vital organization, its offspring, AARP, is much larger with a membership of over 12 million. NRTA as indicated by its name is restricted to schoolteachers, whereas AARP embraces everyone age 55 or over.

Early in AARP's history, and responsible for its tremendous growth, was the know-how and financial support of an insurance company, which by aggressively advertising and selling insurance to members of AARP, also directly and indirectly solicited membership applications. The AARP insurance programs are now larger in premium income than the total premium income of most of the life insurance companies. Members accept AARP's endorsement as a guarantee that the policies are as good or better than offered by any other insurance company—a responsibility that should not be taken lightly by AARP's officers, since AARP freely admits that it receives substantial monies from its insurance carriers. No organization of this magnitude is without its critics who question the aggressiveness and exclusivity of the insurers.

Membership proves to be a bonanza for any lonely person who is thus assured of receiving a steady avalanche of *urgent* hospital and auto insurance literature. I agree with AARP's position that profit-motivated private insurance companies should provide that coverage, rather than ask deficit-spending Washington to do so—but I personally dislike the hard sell and the scare tone of its sales material.

The AARP now has a mailing list of such a size that it is probably only surpassed by the Social Security mailing list. This captive mailing list has a commercial value of many millions of dollars. AARP dues of only $3 per year must produce 20 to 30 million dollars, which could be quite a war chest. So it is no surprise that this tax-exempt non-profit organization is recognized by our elected officials as the most powerful political spokesman for the Senior Citizen.

I am not anti AARP (I am a member) but I tremble when I think of their power potential. I am in favor of their efforts to protect the interests of their members, but I am afraid that they might mis-use their clout to further the interests of the Senior Citizen at the expense of all our other citizens—and especially my grandchildren.

There are many dedicated members working on meri-

torious projects sponsored by this organization. And AARP
has been, and is a major factor, in having furthered the
science of Gerontology. I commend them for their many con-
tributions, but this over 12,000,000 member organization
must accept its responsibility, and never press legislation for
programs that are selfishly oriented, economically unsound,
and a threat to the fiscal soundness of our Social Security
system, our private pension plans, and our nation as a whole.

> As a floor under the retirement incomes of American citi-
> zens, the idea of Social Security has merit; as a steadily
> burgeoning bonanza bestowed on the aged as a device for
> securing their increasingly numerous and increasingly self-
> interested votes, Social Security is a genuine and growing
> threat to the security of society.
>
>   DANIEL ORR
>   Professor of Economics
>   University of California
>   San Diego

* * * * * * * * * * * * * *

Harnessing and directing Senior Citizen political muscle
is the express goal of a newer, more pugnacious movement
started in 1970, called the Gray Panthers.

It began, as all political movements, with one person
who thought she was wronged. Her name, Margaret Kuhn,
but she fights under the name of Maggie Kuhn. The wrong
done her by the establishment was that she was mandatori-
ly retired and she didn't want to go. Her employer incidentally was not a member of the insensitive callous industrial
system, but was the United Presbyterian Office of Church
and Race in New York. So it is no surprise that the abolishment of mandatory retirement is No. One on the Gray
Panthers' Hit Parade.

This demure feisty, mild speaking sharp tongued,

seventyish youngish woman, is great news copy. She doesn't need a public relations advance agent, for the news media spreads her every word to the senior citizens, and they read and listen and join. Pied Piper of the oldies—and the youngsters, too.

From an original founding group of only six persons in 1970 (all of whom were retirees from various national religious and social service organizations) the Gray Panthers, without any formal membership drive, now number thousands. Unlike the AARP, this movement does not have the assistance of an insurance company (although I am certain they are already knocking on Maggie's door). It really doesn't need it, for it has the support of the news media. The publicity and TV exposure given Ms. Kuhn and many of her more articulate followers, would cost more than any commercial organization could afford. And as long as the GP's are untainted by commercialism, they will continue to get free media space, and continue to grow.

Their issues in 1970 seemed to be mainly anti-mandatory retirement, anti-war, and anti-draft. Nothing spectacular occurred until May 1972, when the name "Gray Panthers" appeared somewhere, somehow, and a feature story by Associated Press, New York Times, Washington Star, etc., promoted the name's controversial implication. Maggie Kuhn accepted the challenge and the name.

Without this big news break, the Gray Panthers would be just one more of the many local Senior Citizen Clubs, but with the news media as its sponsor, the Gray Panthers movement is destined to be second only to AARP in size—and may even crowd AARP out of its No. One spot.

Welfare recipients especially find the Gray Panthers to be more promising than the AARP. They are attracted by the GP's action in the unswerving direction of what is good for the older persons—and the youth—is good for the country.

(At this point, I wish the band would play "It Ain't Necessarily So.") AARP is establishment, according to many Gray Panthers, and therefore unable to lead the Seniors to the Promised Land.

In 1973, the Gray Panthers took over or merged with the Retired Professional Action Group, one of Ralph Nader's public citizen groups. When two top controversial media subjects get together, you may be certain you haven't heard the last of either of them.

It is interesting to note the expansion of the GP's issues. On a national level, they are involved in health care; food; inflation; unemployment; housing; transportation; and of course, mandatory retirement (which they condemn as age discrimination). To prove their unselfishness, they are also concerned with age discrimination against the young, who they say, are refused employment because of the youth's age and lack of experience. (I can't resist pointing to the inconsistency. If they are concerned about youth's lack of experience, why are they also against retirement at 65 to make more jobs available to the youth?)

Young people are welcome as members, especially college students, many of whom are enrolled in the new field of study of ageism called Gerontology. And some join because of the promise of action for social change, and the chance to picket in safety under Gramma's immunity. But the middle-aged are *not* courted—they are actually disclaimed as being tied to the abhorred establishment.

From the very beginning, the Gray Panthers have boasted that they were different, definitely not establishment, for they did not collect dues nor issue membership cards nor defer to any GP president. But as they grow in numbers, dues will be a necessity, for they too will become big business. Mailings to thousands of members cost money, and their membership mailing list will be worth money, if rented out to companies selling vitamins, insurance, hearing aids, retirement communal housing, etc. And then they will be offered a percentage of the hearing aid sales, and they will have to decide whether to partake of such establishment practices.

The informality of GP's membership and affilate groups also caught the eye of the media. A group of members is called a *network* and the president or chairman of the meeting is called a *convener.* Any individual may join a network and any five individuals may form a network.

The local networks are encouraged to get involved in local issues—and they do. For example, an elderly man who walked with difficulty was ticketed by a policeman for walking in a cross walk against a red light. I was at a network meeting when this was brought to the attention of the group, as an issue in which all members should be involved. The police were castigated and ridiculed by speaker after speaker. I cringed, wondering the effect such language and disrespect of police would have on the young people who were present. I was pleased when one somber little lady suggested, "Perhaps the man did not wait for the light to turn green. Perhaps he started late when the green was half gone, or on the yellow. I've seen many of our seniors cross streets without looking at the lights. Shouldn't we try to educate our peers to wait for a full green cycle?" But she was shouted down. Here was a cause that was exciting, and as one member noted, worthy of a news story, for no damn greedy cop was going to hassle an oldster and get away with it.

The next night I attended another network meeting in another part of the city, and they had the issue of the same old man and the same damn cop on the agenda—with the same enthusiastic reception as a new cause for action.

Yes, the seniors are getting involved. They have discovered the power of a dozen grandmothers and grandfathers picketing City Hall with the assurance that the TV cameras will be there (for they will have alerted them) and they are sure to be on the five o'clock news.

They will even bite the hand that feeds them, for they are also anti-certain-TV shows—they call their project Media Watch. This is really partisan censorship. They say they don't want TV showing older people in a demeaning fashion, and this includes commercials. For example, they object to the "silly old man squeezing the toilet tissue." (I did not think he was an *old* man, and I'll bet he enjoys squeezing the dollars he is paid.) They object to Johnny Carson's portrayal of "Aunt Blabbie," but they can't be too rough on him because he is responsible for spreading the gospel, as Maggie has been featured on his show.

The future presents a confusing and promising and scary picture. Young people and old people combining forces present an awesome coalition. They can stop rail-roads, fire trucks, building projects, civic meetings. If old folks and kids picket any place at any time—who will be the first policeman or militia who will fire on them, or lay a hand on one of them?

Neither of these age groups give a damn because they don't have any jobs to jeopardize, no employers to antago-nize, and they boast that they have nothing to lose. Note that they disclaim the middle-age group because they have jobs and employers (thus they do have something to lose) and that is why they are ridiculed as the establishment.

I hope that as the GP organization matures it may be-come more balanced, but the meetings I attended allowed no debate on any issue, except when to serve the coffee. Every issue seemed to be for *more* for the seniors without cost to them. There was no other reason for the networks meeting. They voted for whatever they were told they were for—and they voted against whatever the convener said they were against. Never did they consider the cost, for the cost will be borne by the middle-age (*their* children and grandchildren) group, who are not invited to join the Gray Panthers.

I must confess that I was caught red-handed at a GP meeting when I was handed a Petition For Rent Control and I passed it on to the Panther seated next to me. A spy loudly proclaimed to the convener that I had not signed the petition. That stopped the meeting cold. Mr. Convener asked why I had not signed. I answered, "Your petition condemns all landlords. I am a landlord—a decent, fair landlord. I would like to hear some discussion on this petition." And a dear, sweet, sensible lady spoke up, "I would also like to hear this discussed because I have a good landlord, and I would hate to do anything to hurt him." The convener couldn't tolerate such impudence, so he announced that it was obvious that I was not a Gray Panther at heart for I was a capitalist, and he cautioned me, "We Gray Panthers are not reformers—that takes too much time. We are activists!"

I acknowledge that there are unselfish endeavors in which some of the networks are involved, and which excited me so that I rushed to join their ranks. A most notable example of such unselfish service is in the nursing home area. They initiated a course of study for staff members of convalescent and nursing homes, which gives back to the patients one of the most important of their losses—their DIGNITY. Staff members tend to refer to all elderly patients as Mom or Pop, or Jennie or Bennie. The Gray Panthers are given the credit for educating the staff that when service personnel call their patients Mom or Pop, it is demeaning—they have surnames, and should be addressed as Mr. Baker or Mrs. Thompson. Does it really matter? You bet it does!

So this is not a condemnation of the Gray Panthers— it is more in the nature of a prayer. I admit that their growth will be phenomenal and their appeal hypnotic. This is an alert that the Gray Panthers can do anything they set out to do. If they team up with AARP (as they already do on certain issues) they have enough voting power to put Maggie Kuhn in the White House; triple Social Security benefits; pay unemployment benefits to displaced homemakers ; and walk across any city street against the red light.

They can make America a better place for themselves, their children and grandchildren—or they can make it a gravy train for Senior Citizens—BUT THEY CANNOT DO BOTH.

* * * * * * * * * * * * * *

It is with the knowledge and appreciation that the muscle power of the NRTA-AARP and the Gray Panthers can influence legislation to establish an American national health care plan that I especially direct the next two chapters to them.

With their sponsorship, a plan benefiting all age groups, young, middle-aged, and elderly can be formulated to remove from all U.S. citizens the fear of pauperism due to medical and hospital costs.

CHAPTER XXII

FEAR OF PHYSICAL DISABILITY
best be rich or be poor

The fear of physical disability is common to all, but becomes more intense as a person gets older. No matter what your station in life—bank president or bank teller, wealthy, poor, white or black—if you live long enough (or too long, some will say) your legs will peter out and you will be impaired.

Life is a perfect circle. Starting at birth, we go through a short period of physical dependency until we can walk alone unassisted; the second and longest period by far, when we can walk alone, be productive, and assist others to walk; the third, short and last period, when we have completed the circle and are again unable to walk unassisted. And although mercifully, only a few will experience the last period, we are all concerned that we might. (Only 3% of our elderly are in total-care institutions, so 97 to three are pretty good odds that *you won't.*)

The best pre-retirement planning is of little use in the event of catastrophic physical illness. I can only prescribe that it would then be best that you either be in the top money group or in the bottom money group. Either be a rich man or a poor man, for these are the only two classes in our affluent society who can afford our present day medical and hospital costs. The Senior Citizen has some peace of mind, once he is eligible for Medicare. But the productive young, middle-age, and middle-income groups are the most affected. Since they are neither subsidized by welfare nor yet eligible for Medicare, they are not only stuck with their own medical bill, but must also pay the bills incurred by all the others.

I do not believe that people fear catastrophic illness or disability because of the dread of physical pain. That is only something that happens to someone else (until it happens to us) and modern medicine can subdue pain. We are however ALL fearful of physical disability because of the certainty of financial bankruptcy, so vividly advertised by BLUE CROSS, AARP, and the *happy* government scorekeepers. The galloping inflation of medical and hospital care is featured daily by the media and results in an ever-growing antagonism against the *gouging* physicians and hospital administrators.

It is shameful that no one can relax in a state of financial security when constantly reminded that we are subject to the catastrophic costs of a catastrophic illness. A crippled child, open heart surgery, or a stroke can make a pauper out of anyone. And especially for retirees—it is the "Sword of Damocles" over their heads. This horrible fear sometimes turns a senior into a recluse, living in poverty with $100,000 or more in savings accounts—found after death.

How can anyone retire with any peace of mind when his life savings of $25,000; $50,000; $100,000; $300,000; or $500,000 can be wiped out by the nightmarish catastrophic financial demands of modern medicine—which has blessed us with longer life expectancy and doomed us with pauperism if we live so long.

* * * * * * * * * * * * * *

A nation that can afford to send people through outer space should be able to afford to solve its earthly problems.

Let us agree that we have the right to medical and hospital care at time of need—regardless of ability to pay at time of need. But let us admit that NO ONE has the right to such care without paying *if he can pay*—otherwise, everyone also has the right to food, clothing, and shelter—without paying.

The solution is not charity, welfare, Medicare or socialized medicine. No democracy can afford a free-for-all national health plan and still retain its democratic principles.

I admit that unless another solution is proposed soon, we might end up with socialized medicine, for there are more voters who are NOT physicians, than are. It's just as simple as that—VOTES. And when the voters want *free* rent, or *free* plumbing, or *free* eye glasses—it will be so—because there are more voters who are NOT landlords, or who are NOT plumbers, or who are NOT opticians—than are.

BUT THE VOTER'S MIGHT IS NOT NECESSARILY RIGHT!

If the voters have so much clout, why has it taken so long for our legislators to legislate a National Health Plan? Because they know that despite the pressure groups, most voters realize that the cost of a free health care system will bankrupt our economy. Even our most liberal legislators dare not face the risk, for no plan that has been proposed is affordable. Every free plan will escalate in costs to astronomical burdens on the ever-decreasing productive segment of our population.

It is to the credit of our legislators that they have resisted the demand so far, but they are not going to be able to resist much longer. The pressure of organized labor and organized senior citizens are voting blocs that can mow down any resistance. But Thank the Lord, since 1978 we have another very important voting block—the taxpayers—and this new bloc makes serious inroads into (and weakens) the otherwise solid labor and senior citizen blocks.

* * * * * * * * * * * * * *

On June 6, 1978, the passage of Proposition 13 in California signaled the end of the industrial revolution and the beginning of the taxpayer's revolution. Our industrial economic system has failed, for it can no longer cope with the insatiable appetite of the social programmers. The taxpayer's revolution will not disappear but will become ingrained in our economic and political systems. We enter the 1980's which I predict will be known as the Taxpayer's Decade.

No longer will pressure groups to able to force our elected officials to install more *free for some* programs. FOR THE TAXPAYERS HAVE PROCLAIMED THAT NO PROGRAM IS EVER FREE—somebody must pay the tab someday—and that somebody is the taxpayer. The day is gone when legislators can levy taxes without regard to the taxpayer. Proposition 13 is a manifest that from now on, no programs can be legislated without clearly indicating the cost and how the cost is to be met—it can no longer be added to our deficit spending. Of course we will continue to pay taxes to support the promises already made—but we are not going to allow more false and empty promises to be made.

Which means that no national health plan can be promised that adds to inflation and deficit spending through additional taxation or payroll deductions. BUT THIS DOES NOT MEAN WE CANNOT HAVE AN AMERICAN NATIONAL HEALTH CARE PLAN. Instead of increasing taxes, we can solve the problem by DECREASING TAXES—to be specific —TAX SHELTERS.

* * * * * * * * * * * * * *

Tax shelters are composed of EXCESS funds VOLUNTARILY invested by the well-to-do and middle income, and are responsible for a substantial amount of production in such areas as

          Farming
          Cattle
          Oil
          Mining
          Motion pictures
          Commercial property
          Construction
          Housing.

Tax shelters are very important to our economy as they provide risk capital which creates jobs and business activity. Let us establish a tax shelter as an incentive for the well-to-do, and middle income, to voluntarily lend us their excess monies to underwrite a national health care plan for the good of our entire nation.

AND THAT IS WHAT THE NEXT CHAPTER IS ALL ABOUT!

CHAPTER XXIII

INSTANT CREDIT CARD

a tax-sheltered health care plan for life

We have the finest medical and hospital system in the world. Let's keep it—don't destroy it.

It is expensive, too expensive, and becoming more expensive every day, because too much of it is *free to too many,* and has to be *paid-for by too few.*

Although sentiment favors a free socialized cradle-to-grave medical plan (with senior citizens in the forefront)—common sense prevails, and the vast majority of our senior citizens know that a free medical plan for them, is too costly a legacy to leave to their grandchildren.

A recent survey by NBC, of heads of households, re-

ported
      that only 36% favored a National Health plan
           48% voted NO
      and 16% were undecided.

Other polls show that 80 to 85% of the patients are
satisfied with the medical care they receive.

Yet, we must admit that a catastrophic or prolonged
terminal illness, makes every member of the affected family
condemn our entire medical system—because of the horren-
dous money drain.

* * * * * * * * * * * * * *

The American public just doesn't give a damn about the
portion of their bill that is paid by Blue Cross, insurance, or
the government. They don't care and don't even look at the
total of the bill. But they sure scream about the balance—
the amount that comes out of their pockets. Do they scream
at the causes of the over-inflated costs? No! They scream at
the Blue Cross, insurance company, or government for *not
paying the entire bill.*

Prominent people's names are always available as en-
dorsers of any 'screamer's cause, and they will be found
aligned with the socialized medicine activists. But it isn't a
question of socialized medicine. It's only a question of socialized money—someone else's money.

The American public is kidding itself. Blue Cross and
the insurance companies are not paying *their money*—they
are paying *your money.* And if they don't have enough of
your money, they just announce an increase in the premiums
you pay.

And the government, whether federal, state, or local,
has never earned a dime, and hasn't got a dime—it is all tax-

payer's money. (And the taxpayers will soon be a minority group, and they may then be eligible to demand their rights, too.)

As long as the patient has no interest, nor any incentive, to cut the costs of medical and hospital care, we will always have over-utilization, such as unnecessary hospital admittances and the prolonging of hospital stays. We must get the patient involved, so that he is interested in the amount of the total bill, even though he may never be forced to pay it. How? By educating him so that he can understand the problem, and by offering him a solution, that he can also understand.

* * * * * * * * * * * * * *

THE PROBLEM:
Total annual medical/hospital cost *about* . . . . 140 billion*

Paid-for by insurance, Blues, etc., *about* . . . . 33 billion
Paid-for by government (Medicare, etc.), *about*. . . . 50 billion
Paid-for by voluntary non-profit funds, *about*. . . . . . 3 billion

Therefore, it appears that the public out-of-pocket expense is *about*. . . . . 54 billion

*NOTE: Total figure for fiscal year 1975 was only 118.5 billion dollars, according to the National Information Bureau.
For 1976, estimated total costs, from various sources, ranged from 132 billion to 139.9 billion.
Figures that I use, are for illustrative portional purposes, since total figures can never be assumed accurate, and tend to be over-stated. So these figures are yesterdays—tomorrow there will be higher estimates. However the proportions shown above should show very little change.

The 54 billion dollars is what the noise is all about—it is not a 140 billion problem. No one should deny that those who can pay, should—therefore the 54 billion out-of-pocket expense is not a 54 billion hardship—for most of that bill is paid by the people each year.

So let's try to whittle this problem down to its actual size—to the hardship balance of the 54 billion dollars still unpaid, or paid with difficulty.

According to the Congressional Budget Service, nearly 60% of our population is amply covered by insurance or service plans; 34% inadequately covered; and about 8% have no coverage.

The 60% amply covered are usually required to pay 10% to 20% of the bill, as very few have 100% coverage. The 10 to 20% out-of-pocket balances are usually paid without hardship by this group, and this reduces the 54 billion substantially.

The 34% inadequately covered may have to pay out-of-pocket, from 20 to 25% of their incurred medical expenses. And most of them pay their bills. For some, it isn't easy, and for some, it is a real hardship. But this group also pays a large part of their portion of the 54 billion.

The 8% who have no coverage, certainly includes many unemployed, poor, and disadvantaged. Most of this group receive totally free medical care under a government program, and their costs are reflected in the government 50 billion portion.

Therefore, since most of the 54 billion dollars is paid-for by the public out-of-pocket, we should be in agreement that the hardship balance unpaid, is a much smaller figure.

At the end of the year, how much do you think is owed (past due) to physicians and hospitals because of hardship? Let us assume that it is 10%—if so, it is about 5 billion. To be safe, let's say it's an outrageous 20%—that would be about 10 billion. Better yet, let's be ultra-pessimistic and agree on 20 billion—a whopping 37% of 54 billion (much too high, or we would have heard plenty of screaming from the physicians and the hospital administrators).

Now let's take aim at solving the real problem, the *hardship money* problem—the 20 billion problem. Don't wreck the whole medical system. Don't try to come up with 140 billion or 54 billion, when you are only being asked to solve a 20 billion dollar problem.

There is no question but that we should try to help those who cannot pay their out-of-pocket medical expenses. But we should also help those who might be fearful of seriously depleting their reserves of life savings—*a fear, common to ALL OF US.*

* * * * * * * * * * * * * *

Most of the National Health Plans under consideration propose that the government take over the entire 140 billion expense, and add that to the workingman's burden by imposing another compulsory payroll tax (or insurance premium) on both the employee and employer.

What would this accomplish? The payroll tax (or insurance premium) is always added to the cost of the product, and paid by the consumer. So it is inflationary (as if we need more stimulus to inflation). It also removes the incentive for individuals to continue their insurance or Blue Cross coverage —which now provides nearly 25% of the nation's total costs.

* * * * * * * * * * * * * *

I agree with those of our legislators who for the past 30 years, have acknowledged that our over-taxed economy could not support a socialized national health care plan—and today, when our people are demanding tax reductions, it is inconceivable that we can afford such a plan. But we can afford to provide a 20 billion dollar fund, available to any citizen who needs to dip into it for out-of-pocket medical/ hospital costs. And we can afford to create and maintain a solvent fund WITHOUT payroll taxes; WITHOUT compulsory insurance; and WITHOUT adding to inflation. And if we did so, it would solve our national health care problem— the out-of-pocket hardship problem.

* * * * * * * * * * * * * *

THE SOLUTION:
        The Federal Medical Charge Card Plan, composed of
        1. the Federal Medical Charge Card (the CARD) and
        2. the Federal Medical Charge Card Fund (the FUND).

The CARD will allow every U.S. adult citizen to borrow, at 6% annual interest, the amount he needs to pay all or any part of his (or his dependents) *out-of-pocket* medical/ hospital costs, which loan is repayable AFTER death by a lien against the decedent's estate—if he, or she, leaves an estate.

The loans will come from a FUND which will be composed of deposits of excess monies by individuals who will make such deposits voluntarily, *because it pays them to do so,* due to income tax savings *not otherwise available* to them. AND the deposits are guaranteed refundable to the depositors.

This plan means that we do not scuttle what we now have. The insurance companies, Blue Cross, Blue Shield, AARP, HMO's, and the government continue to provide over 60% of the total tab, AND THE FUND provides loans for that part of the out-of-pocket portion that the patient is unable to pay without hardship, and the patient makes that determination—no questions asked.

* * * * * * * * * * * * * *

The FMCC Plan effectively removes the fear of financial annihilation from the minds of our pre-retiree heads of families, and especially from the inflation-whipped minds of our fixed-income retirees. For everyone is painfully aware of the possibility of a castastrophic or terminal illness.

Since the FUND is available to all ages, it will not be a chain-letter windfall for seniors at the expense of the young.

It is an American type of plan. Pay all or part if you can —*none,* if you can't (or won't). And no one will be investigated to determine if he can, or can't (or won't)—until death. Rich or poor—no investigation until death.

The FMCC Plan will assure that no one in our affluent society need suffer or die, due to lack of money for medical or hospital attention. Every U.S. citizen will have a CARD which will provide loans for any part, or all, of his (or his dependents) medical and hospital costs. He does not ever have to exercise the loan privilege, but he can, at any time, regardless of his financial status, as long as it is for the *amount in excess* of insurance or government reimbursement.

This is a LIFETIME LOAN. It will not require thousands of Federal employees or interpretations, or percentage computing, or determining eligibility, such as deciding whether a person is poor or near-poor (as actually required in one proposed plan).

The FMCC Plan permits hospitalization to be authorized by a qualified physician, in an accredited hospital, for any length of time approved by the Utilization Review Committee. At the end of the hospital stay, the patient will be given his bill, which he can pay himself; or by insurance or government reimbursement assignment; or charge to the FUND all or any part of the bill that is NOT covered by insurance or government reimbursement.

Since the doctor and the hospital are guaranteed payment, every CARD holder should receive prompt and adequate medical care.

And never again do I want to read about an elderly
couple who have used up all their savings, and the husband
must get a divorce, so that his sick wife might be eligible for
medical care in accordance with the crazy-quilt rules of our
federal agency programs.

* * * * * * * * * * * * * *

Enough said about the CARD. How do we get the
FUND established with excess monies deposited therein by
individuals on a voluntary basis?

* * * * * * * * * * * * * *

THE FUND
We can create such a FUND quickly and easily by allowing everyone the same tax reduction/tax shelter privilege
now allowed only to a privileged segment of our society.

Among the newest and most rapidly increasing forms of
tax shelters are the Keogh plans (since 1964) and the Individual Retirement Accounts (IRA's—since 1973). These tax
shelters allow certain individuals to skim-off money from
their income each year, provided it is deposited in a Keogh
or IRA account in a bank, savings & loan association, insurance company, etc., and they pay no income tax thereon
until they withdraw their non-taxed monies (after age 59½
but not later than 70½). These are voluntary deposits, within
prescribed limits, primarily for the purpose of allowing
people, who can afford, it, to set aside money for their retirement years. The purpose is laudable, but without the incentive of tax deferment there would be no Keogh or IRA accounts.

Under Keogh—a person who is SELF-EMPLOYED may deduct from his taxable income 15% of his income up to $7500 maximum annually. (Can be $15,000 or more.)*

Under IRA—an EMPLOYEE who is NOT covered by an employer's qualified pension plan, may deduct from his taxable income 15% of his income up to $1500 maximum annually.

Question: Why should a SELF-EMPLOYED be allowed a $7500 deduction, while an employed person (not under a company pension plan) is only allowed $1500? Isn't that discriminatory?

But the thousands who are working for IBM, General Motors, Standard Oil, Sears, Metropolitan Life, etc., cannot deduct $1500 or $15,000 because they are *not* self-employed and they *are* participants in their company qualified pension plan.

Question? Isn't that discriminatory?

Suppose we say to the now privileged Keogh and IRA tax reductioneers, "You can continue to have your tax shelter privilege PROVIDED your deposits, from now on, go into the FMCC FUND." And we also say to *all* people, "You can have the same privilege even though you work for IBM, General Motors, etc.," AND everyone, Keogh, IRA, and IBM and General Motors employees can deposit up to the same maximum and have the same tax reduction privilege.

Question? Isn't this NON-discriminatory?

* * * * * * * * * * * * * *

To eliminate the present discriminatory Keogh and IRA tax shelters, our tax laws would have to be changed to direct that the FUND be the ONLY permissable tax-sheltered de-

*As per IRS regulations issued May 1978—called Defined Benefit. Designed primarily for individuals earning $50,000 or more.

pository for future Keogh and IRA type deposits, and since EVERYONE would be allowed the same tax reduction privilege, there would no longer be any need for Keogh or IRA regulations.

These tax sheltered accounts would thus benefit the entire nation IN ADDITION to benefiting the depositors. (Even as I am in the process of writing this book, bills in Congress are being proposed to expand these tax shelters so that more billions can be "skimmed off" for the exclusive benefit of the fortunate individuals who qualify.)

Today, any interest earned by Keogh and IRA accounts is also non-taxable until withdrawn. We propose that the FUND should pay no interest, but offer as an important offset—NO INCOME TAX on withdrawal of deposits. This latter provision would necessitate establishing a reasonable number of years (such as 10 years) for each deposit to remain in the FUND, in order to qualify for TAX EXEMPTION upon withdrawal.

However, any depositor should be allowed to withdraw his deposits at any time, BUT if before 10 years, he would have to pay income tax on the amount withdrawn.

We should allow early withdrawal with NO INCOME TAX if for an assignment to the FUND in order to pay off a CARD loan.

For example: John Doe has deposited $7500 each year for 4 years to the FUND—total $30,000. He is hospitalized and charged $10,000 out-of-pocket hospital/medical costs to his CARD. Upon recovery he decides to pay off the 6% loan rather than leave it remain a lien to be payable upon death. He assigns the $10,000 (plus interest) to the FUND. Result—he has about $20,000 balance to his credit in the FUND.

* * * * * * * * * * * * * *

Uncollectible liens would NOT be an obligation of other family members (except for surviving spouse's estate).

If the borrower died destitute, the FUND would simply record the entire loan as uncollectible. If he left a small estate, the FUND might collect part of the loan and cancel the uncollectible portion. If the decedent was well-to-do, the FUND would collect its total outlay, plus 6% annual interest. The majority of the middle-income class would leave an estate, and from this group, part or entire restitution would be made. The 6% interest and the interest on the float will help offset some of the uncollectible liens.

The middle-income and well-to-do would have every incentive to purchase or to continue their insurance or Blues coverage, in order that the lien against their estates be minimized. Although the poor or the shiftless do not carry insurance, they still would receive any necessary medical attention, without any inference of charity or welfare.

The cost to the government for any deficit due to uncollectible liens (yes, the government is to reimburse the FUND) would be substantially the same as it is today—or less. For the government today is bearing the costs of Medicaid for 22.9 million poor. They too, would no doubt rather borrow from the FUND, and since many of them will get out of the poor category before they die—the FUND would recover some of the present government's non-recoverable costs. So, it might cost the government less.

Employer and union group insurance or service plans would not only continue, but would expand. That is good, because many of these plans are now paying between 80 to 90% of their portion of our national medical expenditures. For example: One of the Teamsters Union plans pays over

$500,000 each day for its members, and the Ford Motor Co. pays well over 300 million each year.

For those who have no group coverage, or who have inadequate coverage, or who cannot afford an individual insurance policy, or for the retired, the loan privilege spells "peace of mind."

I am not implying that today's Keogh and IRA depositors are *bad guys* or committing a crime against the rest of us—for tax shelter is not tax avoidance. It is only tax deferment until a later date.

The largest class of depositors to Keogh, in my opinion (in relation to the total number in that profession), are physicians. I cannot envision any serious objections from this group to the changes we propose. They would be lending their excess money to a FUND that, in turn, would lend the money to patients to pay their physicians.

There will be some who will say that many Keogh and IRA depositors will refuse to make deposits to a non-interest paying FUND. My answer is—if they don't deposit the Keogh $7500 into the FUND, it's fine with me and all the other taxpayers, since the IRS will collect $3750 (if in the 50% bracket, as most Keoghites are). Try investing the balance of $3750—be sure tax is paid each year on the interest earnings —and see how that compares with a full $7500 in the FUND. The result should make the continuation of Keogh and IRA deposits in the FUND, a most attractive option.

* * * * * * * * * * * * * * *

As deaths of borrowers occur, liens collected from the estates will replenish the FUND. The 6% annual interest, plus the interest on the float (on FUND balances) will help pay for the uncollectible liens and expenses.

Obviously, there will be uncollectible liens, and these losses should be made up to the FUND by the government— which is no different than the government absorbing the medical costs today for the poor and disadvantaged.

It should also be obvious to all that THE GOVERN- MENT'S 50 BILLION SHARE OF THE NATIONS' MEDI- CAL EXPENSES *TODAY, INCLUDES* AND *DUPLICATES* MUCH OF THE UNCOLLECTIBLE LIENS OF THE *FU- TURE.*

* * * * * * * * * * * * *

To thwart the ever present cheaters, we would need to amend our Bankruptcy Laws so that FMCC FUND loans would never be erased by bankruptcy.

And we would have to pass new laws to protect the FMCC FUND, by making property transferred *without full and adequate consideration* within five (or maybe six or seven) years of death, liable for repayment to the FUND.

* * * * * * * * * * * * *

There would be an incentive for many people to repay loans prior to death, because everyone should be allowed to deduct the repayment of such loan from *any year's income.* For example: John Doe owes $12,000 which was incurred during his family up-bringing years. He has now become suc- cessful and his income is subject to a 60% Income Tax at the top. So he pays off the $12,000 loan, which is deduct- ible, therefore it costs him only $4800.

Another example: Bob Smith is an executive earning $65,000 annually. He is going to retire next year on a com- pany pension of $20,000 a year. If he pays off his FUND loan before he retires, it might cost him much less than if it is paid off later by his estate. (And if he should need to borrow again from the FUND later—he is eligible to do so, at any time—so why not take advantage of a tax bargain?)

Tax exemption of life insurance premiums should also be allowed for any policies naming the FMCC FUND as the irrevocable beneficiary for the amount of any FMCC loan at time of death. Any excess would be payable to the heirs (subject to tax adjustments for excess-of-loan premiums).

* * * * * * * * * * * * * * *

The FMCC Plan will tend to reduce the abuse of unnecessary hospitalization, because it is a well-known fact that most people will not be so inclined, when it is charged against their estate.

The problem that charges may increase substantially, due to the FUND paying the bill, must be dealt with by establishing ceilings for all services. For example: Only accredited hospitals could get FMCC payments and for *established ward rates only*. Also, physician's and surgeon's charges would have to be limited. If the ceiling for a specific operation was $500, that is all one could borrow from the FUND. If the surgeon asked $1000, and the patient agreed to pay $1000, the loan from the FUND for $500 would NOT be available, since we would merely be feeding that old Devil called INFLATION.

I appreciate that the American Medical Association and the hospital associations are against controls. So am I! But, when they consider the alternative of socialized medicine, I am certain they will support the FMCC Plan. Physicians and hospitals would not be prevented from charging more than the ceilings to anyone who would pay it. But if the FUND is to pay the money, then the loans must be subject to reasonable ceilings and controls.

Many of us would be both lenders *and* borrowers under

the FMCC Plan. So we would have a double incentive to police our own utilization of medical and hospital service, and have more than a passing interest in the costs.

There will be immediate protests by some who will be upset by the idea of a lien on the estate, claiming that this might wipe out the estate that would otherwise be left to the grief-stricken widow. So, let's be prepared to wait until the bona-fide widow, or widower, passes on.

* * * * * * * * * * * * *

It is difficult to be practical and emotional at the same time. The government has no obligation to guarantee that every citizen will have an estate to be left to his heirs—without first paying his obligations. I am prepared for such criticism and will admit that some estates will be wiped out. May I point out that—if wiped out by the FUND lien—there never was an estate to be heired. The FMCC Plan deserves praise rather than criticism, for it allows a person to enjoy his (otherwise bankrupt) estate until his death—after which I doubt that he is too concerned.

The FMCC Plan is a solution that must be acceptable to the proponents of all the other proposed plans. For all plans say the same thing—they have but one objective, and that is—to guarantee that everyone, regardless of financial ability, will have access to medical and hospital care. The FMCC Plan does that!

* * * * * * * * * * * * *

The administration of any national program has always lead to more bureaucracy. And this national health care plan could result in many thousands of additional public employees with attendant ever-increasing salaries, pensions, etc., which could destroy the non-inflationary aims of the FMCC Plan.

Instead, let us make use of the experience and expertise of our vast untapped national resource—our senior citizens. They can fill the thousands of positions created by the FMCC Plan, at nominal salaries, without the stigma of under-cutting minimum hourly wage laws, or displacing existing employees —for this should be viewed as a social service. Obviously, we will need Federal subsidies for the installation and operation of the Plan, but the utilization of senior citizens, and allowing them additional income opportunities, will also remove thousands of them from our welfare and financial assistance programs—thus offsetting a substantial sum now being expended upon those programs.

At present, we solicit senior citizens to join the Peace Corps to assist foreign countries. Certainly they would respond to the same altruistic appeal to assist their own country.

* * * * * * * * * * * * * *

Therefore, I propose that the operation of the sacred trust FUNDed Plan be controlled by a National Board of Trustees, and local Community Boards of Trustees, composed of

MEN AND WOMEN WHO HAVE RETIRED

from the fields of medicine, hospital institutions, insurance, Blue Cross, labor unions, banks, savings and loan institutions, credit unions, education, NRTA-AARP, Gray Panthers, and last but definitely not least—government (especially ex-elected public officials).

I visualize local Community Boards of Trusteees throughout the country (similar to the Draft Boards of war years) all working for the same nominal salary—say, $250 a month. (We would need a special exemption from the minimum hourly wage law.)

This would mean that we are not adding public employees. No Civil Service. No pension or fringe benefits. No perpetuity in employment. No union representation. No strikes. But I do ask for one special (tax-sheltered) tax concession for these civic-minded Trustees—their $250 monthly salaries should not be taxable, but be tax-free income, same as Social Security income.

So, we have the money and the staff. Now, how will the FMCC Plan be received by our young, middle-aged, and seniors? (Anyone else, I confess, I care nothing about.)

* * * * * * * * * * * * * *

The vast majority will favor the FMCC Plan, because it benefits all segments of our populace.

1. The poor, underprivileged, and disadvantaged will like it because they get immediate health care without inference of welfare or charity and they might pay for it eventually, if they amass an estate during their lifetime.
2. The middle-income class will like it, because serious illness of any member of the family will not affect their standard of living. This group will be providing a large part of the FUND, since they are participants in Keogh and IRA accounts. And they will tend not to borrow from the FUND, unless for a major expense in excess of their insurance coverage.
3. The well-to-do will like it, because they can get a 6% loan (for amounts in excess of insurance) while they invest their money at a higher interest rate. However, we expect to collect this loan, with interest, from their estate. They, too, would be major lenders to

the FUND, since they are major depositors
to Keogh and IRA.

4. The doctors and hospitals will like it, because there will be less bureaucratic controls
under this Plan, and it removes the threat of
socialized medicine.

5. The insurance companies, Blue Cross, Blue
Shield, and AARP will like it, because it will
enable them to remain in the health insurance
business, and continue their growth.

6. The labor unions will like it, because they can
continue to push for more health insurance,
with the added argument that they don't
want their members to borrow from the
FUND.

7. The employers will like it, because they can
argue that more health insurance coverage is
not essential, since all are now protected
under the FMCC umbrella.

8. The Democrats will like it, because the
poor, under-privileged, disadvantaged, middle-
income, well-to-do, doctors, hospitals, insurance companies, the Blues, AARP, unions and
employers like it.

9. The Republicans will like it, for the same reasons that the Democrats like it.

10. The young, middle-aged, and we, the senior
citizens will like it, because we are all members of the groups listed above, and we can
be solvent for as long as we live—and so can
everyone else.

11. The banks, savings and loan associations,
mutual funds, and insurance companies
WON'T LIKE IT at first. But they always got
along fine without Keogh and IRA, and they
can give up this tax-shelter for the benefit of
the general public.

12. The Socialists WON'T LIKE IT, because we

will be the only industrialized society that can
continue to be industrialized—instead of socialized.

* * * * * * * * * * * * * *

The idea of a lifetime loan payable after death is neither
preposterous nor unusual. It is in effect in nine states, allowing senior citizens to borrow from the state, to pay the property tax levied against their homes. And it is reported that
only a very small percentage of those eligible do borrow—
because people do not tend to abuse the loan privilege.

The idea of creating a fund through voluntary tax-
exempt deposits by some, to provide loans to others, is also
not unique. It has recently been established by the city of
Chicago. This, too, is in relation to homes, providing mort-
gages at lower than prevailing interest rates. And it is spreading throughout the country as other cities are proposing the
same type of program.

If we can provide loans to save a person's home—
shouldn't we provide loans to save a person's life?

* * * * * * * * * * * * * *

Many dedicated fellow Americans from the fields of
government, organized labor, education, medicine, insurance
—people of all ages, but especially senior citizens, NRTA-
AARP members, and Gray Panthers, have unselfishly given
much in time, study, and research to this major problem. But
the question of how to provide the money for a national
health care plan, has been the insurmountable obstacle to the
adoption of any of the proposed plans.

The Federal Medical Charge Card Plan is feasible, practical, and affordable, as it is the only plan whose funding concept does not call for additional inflationary taxation. And,

it is not in conflict with any other proposed program for the delivery of medical/hospital care. If the Kennedy-Waxman Plan, or the President Carter Plan, or the American Medical Association Plan, or any other proposed health plan—if *everyone* of them would incorporate the concept of the FMCC method of funding, you could choose *anyone* of them as your national health plan. For with the incorporation of the FMCC FUND, all proposed plans are acceptable since they all have the same single noble purpose—that of delivering health care without regard to the patient's financial ability to pay, at the time of his need.

And most important—add the FMCC FUND to any plan and there would be no more need to degrade and dehumanize our people by sorting them into groups of OLD and POOR—as every other plan does now propose.

But will the FMCC method of *funding/loaning* solve the problem?

I can prove it will. I can prove it, here and now.

If I could distribute to each one of you a Federal Medical Charge Card TODAY—you would never again, from this moment on, ever fear that you might someday be wiped out financially, due to an unexpected catastrophic *out-of-pocket* medical bill.

CHAPTER XXIV

NOW I AM GOING TO TELL YOU

what I told you

In Chapter I

—I TOLD YOU that people are not things. People are not scrapped when they get older—*things* are!

"RETIRE—to put on a new set of tires." I consider that a proper definition when applied to people. Change of tires/ change of work. But I recommend that one should change his tires while he/she is still able to drive.

In Chapter II

—I TOLD YOU that getting older was easy—just keep breathing. Getting smarter as one gets older is what this is all about. Don't believe the age statistics and more important, don't be one. Retirement is the time when you take over and you become skipper of your own ship. Being a skipper for 30% of your lifetime can be a pleasant cruise, or a miserable lost at sea misadventure. You're the skipper.

In Chapter III
—I TOLD YOU that re*TI*re*ME*nt is TIME: Time to work, doing what you always said you wanted to do, could do, and would do, if you had the TIME.

If you meant it, do it. If not, quit griping. And if you are one of the fortunate few who enjoy what you have been working at, then by all means, continue baking those bagels or conducting that symphony orchestra.

In Chapter IV
—I TOLD YOU that planning and worrying are not the same. Pre-retirement planning is the way to eliminate post-retirement worrying.

Plan for living, but never worry about LIFE, for you'll never get out of it alive, anyway.

In Chapter V
—I TOLD YOU that you should PLAY THE 65 GAME. But there is no law *yet* against playing it at 55, 60, or 62. The game is the same—only the players change. It costs no money to play the game, but it might cost you a lot if you don't play it.

In Chapter VI
—I TOLD YOU that someone out there needs you, and someone always will. So long as this is true you cannot give me that old excuse that you are lonely, bored, and can't find anything to do—unless you are a bore, and don't want anything to do.

In Chapter VII
—I TOLD YOU that you should retire early while you may,

for early retirees live sooner and longer. Over 50% of our Social Securitants are early retirees, and they aren't about to leave while the checks are coming in. So they are going to set new highs for life expectancy, which is good for them but bad for the S.S. fund. The government should consider moving the Social Security retirement age up to 68 or 70. Don't worry—it has already been suggested, but they know you won't let them do it.

In Chapter VIII
—I TOLD YOU that looking forward to retiring is fine but don't stop there—look beyond your retirement day and plan what you will do the next day, week, month, year and years.

I hope that this book will convince many more to retire earlier to begin a second career, while they still can. I claim that dread of retirement is not a legitimate fear, but an excuse. Soon the majority will be retired, so why not join the Club when *you* want to. It's free and your dues are paid. Otherwise, the Club will notify you when you *must* join and there may be a penalty of additional dues for late joiners.

In Chapter IX
—I TOLD YOU that an executive is a person who lives two lives—his business life where he is SOMEBODY, and his home life where he is ANYBODY. You should realize that being ANYBODY is not so bad, really; it's only bad when you become a NOBODY.

Retirement doesn't make a SOMEBODY a NOBODY. Nobody but you can do that to you.

In Chapter X
—I TOLD YOU that anyone who can and wants to work can find work.

Jobs are not always available, but work always is.

In Chapter XI
—I TOLD YOU that you are NOT SUDDENLY 55, 60, or 65 on your retirement day. You are exactly ONE DAY OLDER than the day before. Retirement does not mean OLD. Retirement means NEW.

I also said that many of you will develop aches and allergies that you have always had but never before noticed. Try this experiment. Sit at home alone in complete solitude and quiet. (Shut the boob tube off.) Now concentrate on the noise. Listen to the hum of the refrigerator; the ticking of the clock; the roar of the autos and trucks and the ear-splitting motorcycle; the barking dog; the neighbor screaming at her child; the noises of life and living can drive you nuts—if you concentrate on listening. The noise has always been there but you never noticed it before. Same with your aches and allergies.

If you retire to do nothing but sit and concentrate on your own miserable self, you'll discover all your aches and you'll drive the doctor nuts.

So my advice is that if you are going to be a sitter, concentrate on the noise instead of yourself, and you will soon become active fighting City Hall to do something about the noise pollution.

In Chapter XII
—I TOLD YOU that it is tough when a long-time couple becomes a single due to death, and it can seem like the end of the world to the surviving partner. My advice to the grieving spouse is, "Don't spread the pain to your loved ones. It is very personally yours to bear. Your grief will pass and life will go on, with or without you—better, with you."

In Chapter XIII
—I TOLD YOU that the question of the time for a total-care institution is one that tears families asunder. But it is

no different than the question of hospitalization—a necessity at some time.

Although a spouse will often care for a partner who cannot tend to his or her own personal needs, it is many times carried to the point of physical impairment of the caretaker. That is of no use to either party.

I hope I do not offend many lovely people who are devotedly caring for elderly invalids. Your devotion is noble, but if it becomes a physical sacrifice, perhaps you should be reminded—you too, have only one life to live, and who would you look to, if you were unable to care for yourself?

In Chapter XIV
—I TOLD YOU that the status of homemaking should be raised from the old school Home Economics level to at least the same level as typing, bookkeeping, keypunch operator. What I tried to say, without offending women (because some of my best friends are women) don't change DISplaced homemakers into MISplaced homemakers.

In Chapter XV
—I TOLD YOU that legislated rights are not always right. If they must be legislated FOR someone, they must be AGAINST someone. When its application proves to create more wrongs than rights, common sense should prevail. I am referring to the nitpicking rights. For example: Most newspapers are now ignoring the classified ad sex taboo, when it is obvious that a motherless family is not in the market for another father.

In Chapter XVI
—I TOLD YOU I agree that man should work until he can no longer, or wants no longer to work. But I am against forcing an employer to keep him on the job when the employee can no longer perform his duties adequately. I don't believe in passing laws for emotional and moral reasons that solve

the problems of a few, at the expense of many.

In Chapter XVII
—I TOLD YOU that a money-needing-senior should sell his
home if, as in most cases, it will improve his financial situation. To facilitate the sale at a top price, the seller should
consider being the mortgagee at the current high rate of interest. For a senior, collecting monthly payments over a 20
to 30 year period, is tantamount to having an annuity.

In Chapter XVIII
—I TOLD YOU that I'm not slamming the Leisure World
type of community living any more than I would slam a first
class cruise around the world. I think it's great. Since it is
expensive, it is not going to be a major factor in solving the
senior (or others in need) citizen housing problem, unless
government decides to build Leisure Worlds all over the
country. This might solve the senior citizen problem and give
the problem to the junior citizens.

In Chapter XIX
—I TOLD YOU that I am convinced that, dollar for dollar,
the mobile home is by far the best buy as a permanent residence, especially for retirees who wish to reduce expenses.
Many people have sold their immobile homes for $40,000 to
$100,000, and have purchased more luxurious mobile homes
for $15,000 to $30,000.

In Chapter XX
—I TOLD YOU that it's ironical how inflation makes hypo-
crites out of otherwise reasonable people. Among the loudest
advocates for rent control are senior citizens. Those, whose
major income is Social Security I can understand and forgive.
But, those who just sold their homes and received $100,000
for their $10,000 home have no business picketing and carry-
ing signs for rent control. Sure, rents have increased, but not
nearly as much as postage stamps, or McDonalds hamburgers,
and certainly not as much as the selling price of a single
home.

Let's face facts. Today if the public had a chance to vote FOR INFLATION or DEFLATION—INFLATION would win because the people on fixed incomes haven't gotten mad as hell yet. So learn to live with it for a while longer since it won't go away as long as you like it. But when public employee under-funded pension plans are forced to forego any more cost-of-living increases, and when Social Security retirement benefits are frozen with no more automatic increases—INFLATION will be stopped because YOU, and the public employees, and every person who ever expects to collect Social Security WON'T LIKE it any longer.

In Chapter XXI

—I TOLD YOU that the American Association of Retired Persons (AARP) owed much of its spectacular growth to the sales expertise and financial support of an insurance company, and that for many years there has been criticism of this exclusive alliance.

In 1979, AARP announced that its insurance contracts with the Colonial Penn Insurance Group would be allowed to expire in 1981, and that AARP would concentrate on their essential tasks of representing all older Americans.

DOES THIS MEAN THAT AARP WILL EMERGE AS THE THIRD MAJOR POLITICAL PARTY?

In Chapter XXII

—I TOLD YOU that old age has never killed anyone. It takes disease or an accident to kill anyone at any age. And the odds are 97 to three that you will live the rest of your life.

Fear of the financial ravages caused by catastrophic illness is common to me, you, and all of us. I believe that we could be relieved of that common fear if we were assured that we might have the money we need when we need it—to be repaid by us whenever we wished or when we no longer had any need for any money.

AND I BELIEVE SUCH ASSURANCE IS POSSIBLE!

In Chapter XXIII

—I TOLD YOU that the proponents have only one argument in favor of socialized medicine. They claim that the U.S. is the only industrialized nation without free socialized medicine. Therefore we are a backward country in respect to the rights of our citizens.

Then how come if we are so backward, that an overwhelming number of citizens from those enlightened socialized countries are trying to emigrate to the U.S.? If we did not have quotas we would have half the world's population within our borders. How come those other countries have no need for quotas limiting Americans who should be clamoring to live in their promised lands? Why aren't U.S. citizens lining up to migrate to the countries who have free medicine? How come? Is it possible that Americans still value individual freedom above all else? Yes, it is—for AMERICA is spelt F R E E D O M.

In Chapter XXIV

—I TOLD YOU what I had told you, and some things that I had forgotten to tell you

THAT IS WHAT I TOLD YOU

and if you listened, you would know that though this might be

THE END

it could be a new beginning.

Epilogue

I was most fortunate to have been blessed with a group of friends who encouraged me to retire—each time I retired. For 23 years, they were a supportive audience while I climbed the executive ladder, and retired from insurance company chief executive; to consultant; to income property owner/operator; to my present career as an author.

Most people think that writing is a lonely and very private profession. But I am not a disciplined reclusive furtive, secretive writer who labors for years in seclusion, and then suddenly announces the birth of his book. I am an anticipator—and without an audience throughout my gestation period, I could never bring my pregnancy to a successful conclusion. For the past 3 years, the Tennet Associates have listened to my readings of this book as it developed—chapter by chapter; and I benefited by their approvals and criticisms, as I rewrote, changed, modified, discarded and embellished.

I wish to acknowledge my deep appreciation to my fellow members of the Tennet Associates: Mildred Bashook, Dr. Gerald and Myrna Bernath, Dr. Allen and Dorothy Brodwin, Jacob and Anne Entin, Dr. Reuben and Lillian Kaufman, Samuel and Florence Lutwick, and Joseph and Millie Youtan.

I am also indebted to the audiences who attended my speaking engagements, where I projected and tested various segments of this book—especially the Federal Medical Charge Card Plan.

And now, as a mother must one day let go of her child's hand so that he can walk alone—I too, must let go of my book—with love.

Joseph Schwartz

Index

AARP (American Association of Retired Persons) 171-174
AARP hospital insurance 43-47
Abolishment of mandatory retirement 129-134
ACTION 56-58
Alliance of Displaced Homemakers 114-117

Andrus, Ethel Percy 172
Apartment building manager 90
Apartment business 85, 143, 144
Apartment living 142
Attitudes 37, 38

Bank guard 89
Boredom 55, 56

Causistic medicine 97-100
CETA (Comprehensive Employment Training Act) 165
Commission sales 90-92
Consultant opportunities 82, 83
Coupon clipping 169

Definition of 'retirement' 11-14
Department store employment 89
Direct selling opportunities 91, 92
Disability 181-183
Discrimination 121-127
Displaced homemakers 114-117; 121-125
Dread of retirement 76

Early retirement (employer pension plan) 68, 81
Early retirement (Social Security) 66-69
Environmental Fund 20
Equality 15, 16
Executives 79-86
Expectancy of life 21-23

Fear of retirement 18, 76
Federal Medical Charge Card Plan (FMCC) 187-206
Financial fear 33, 39-54
Financial planning 39-53
FMCC Board of Trustees 202, 203
FMCC Card 187-206
FMCC Fund 194-206
Foster grandparents (FGP) 56

Government statistics 19, 20, 22, 163
Gray Panthers 174-180

Health (hospital) insurance 41-47
Homemakers 114-119; 121-125
Housing
    Apartment living 142
    Condominiums 145
    Home-sharing 145
    Mobile homes 155-159
    Retirement communities 147-153
    Single homes 137-145

Income property 85, 143, 144
Inflation 161-170, 213
Insurance, health 41-47
Insurance, life 47-53, 200
IRA(individual retirement annuity) 194-198

Keogh Plan 194-198
Kuhn, Margaret 174

Leisure World 147-150
Life expectancy 21-23
Life expectancy of executives 83
Life Insurance 47-53, 200
Living in a child's home 103-112
Loans to children 104, 105
Loneliness 55, 56

Managing apartment buildings 90
Mandatory retirement 129-134
Media watch 178
Military pensions 35-37, 63
Minimum hourly wage 164-166
Mobile homes 155-159

National health plan 183-206
NCVA (National Center for Voluntary Action) 58
Non-forfeiture values 47-53
NRTA (National Retired Teachers Association 172

Orr, Daniel 174

Peace Corps 56
Phase-out salary plan 81
Physical disability medical cost fears 181-185